TEACHER'S PET PUBLICATIONS

PUZZLE PACK
for
The Indian in the Cupboard

based on the book by
Lynn Reid Banks

Written by
Mary B. Collins

© 2008 Teacher's Pet Publications
All Rights Reserved

The materials in this packet are copyrighted
by Teacher's Pet Publications, Inc.

These pages may be duplicated by the purchaser
for use in the purchaser's own classroom.

Copying any of these materials and distributing them
for any other purpose is a violation of the copyright laws.

© 2008 Teacher's Pet Publications, Inc.
www.tpet.com

INTRODUCTION
If you already own the LitPlan for this title, this Puzzle Pack will refresh your Unit Resource Materials and Vocabulary Resource Materials sections plus give you additional materials you can substitute into the tests. If you do not already have a complete LitPlan, these pages will give you some supplemental materials to use with your own plan. There are two main groups of materials: one set for unit words (such as characters' names, symbols, places, etc.) and one set for vocabulary words associated with the book.

WORD LIST
There is a word list for both the unit words and the vocabulary words. These lists show you which words are being used in the materials and the clues or definitions being used for those words. You may want to give students a word list with clues/definitions to help them, or you may want students to only have a word list (without clues/definitions) if you want them to work a little harder. Both are available for duplication. The word lists can also be your "calling key" for the bingo games.

FILL IN THE BLANK AND MATCHING
There are 4 each of the fill in the blank and matching worksheets for both the unit and vocabulary words. These pages can be used either as extra worksheets for students or as objective parts of a unit test. They can be done individually if students need extra help or as a whole class activity to review the material covered.

MAGIC SQUARES
The magic squares not only reinforce the material covered but also work on reasoning and math skills. Many teachers have told us that their students really enjoy doing these!

WORD SEARCH PUZZLES
The word search words go in all directions, as indicated on your answer keys. Two of the word search puzzles have the clues listed rather than the words. This makes the puzzle a little more difficult, but it reinforces the material better. Two word search puzzles have words only for students who find the clue puzzles too difficult.

CROSSWORD PUZZLES
Both unit and vocabulary word sections have 4 crossword puzzles.

BINGO CARDS
There are 32 individual bingo cards for the unit words and 32 individual bingo cards for the vocabulary words. You can use your word list as a "call list," calling the words at random and marking them off of your list as you go, or you could use the flash cards by cutting them apart and drawing the words at random from a hat (or box or whatever). To make a better review, you might ask for the definition and spelling of each word as you call it out–or you could call out the definitions and have students tell you the words they need to look for on the puzzle.

JUGGLE LETTERS
The vocabulary juggle letter game is intended to help students learn the spellings of the words. One sheet has the definitions listed on it as an extra help for students who need it or to reinforce the definitions if you choose to do so.

FLASH CARDS
We've included a set of vocabulary flash cards you can duplicate, cut, and fold for your students. Some teachers make a few sets for general use by the class; others make a set for each student. Some teachers duplicate them for each student and have the students cut & fold their own. You can cut out just the words and put them in a hat, have each student pick out one word and write the definition and a sentence for that word. Students then swap words and papers, with the next student adding a sentence of his own under the last one. You can have students swap as many times as you like. Each time the student will read the sentences written prior to his own and then add a sentence. You can cut out the words and definitions separately and play "I Have; Who Has?" Each student in the room draws a word and definition. The first student says, "I have (the name of the word). Who has the definition?" The student with the definition reads it then says, "I have (the name of the vocabulary word she has). Who has the definition?" The round continues until all words and definitions have been given.

Indian In The Cupboard Word List

No.	Word	Clue/Definition
1.	ADIEL	Omri's brother with the missing football shorts
2.	APRIL	Girl who teases Patrick at school
3.	ARROW	Little Bear removes this from Boone's chest.
4.	ART	Boone's best subject in school
5.	BANDAGE	What Omri needs from the medical orderly
6.	BEAR	Indian in the cupboard: Little _____
7.	BEARD	Slang for
8.	BEEF	Omri gave Little Bear canned _____ for breakfast.
9.	BELT	Little Bear gave Omri this as payment for his wife.
10.	BLOOD	Little Bear and Omri; Little Bear and Boone are _____ Brothers
11.	BOOHOO	Boone's nickname
12.	BOONE	Plastic cowboy who comes to life
13.	BOW	Belonged to the dead Indian chief
14.	CHAIN	Omri's mother plans to keep the key on this
15.	CHIEF	He died inside the cupboard: Indian _____.
16.	COKE	Drink Omri gave the Indian
17.	COWBOY	Omri was afraid Little Bear would kill him.
18.	CRIES	Reason for Boone's nickname
19.	CUPBOARD	Place where toys come to life
20.	DREAM	The soldier thinks Omri is a _____.
21.	EGG	Used as a wash basin for Boone & Little Bear: _____ cup
22.	GILLON	Omri's brother who gave Omri the cupboard
23.	HAIL	It was the size of a football to Little Bear and Boone.
24.	HALLUCY	Boone's nickname for Omri: _____-Nation
25.	HEADDRESS	Little Bear destroys this
26.	INDIAN	Patrick's birthday gift to Omri: Plastic _____
27.	IROQUOIS	Little Bear belonged to this tribe.
28.	JOHNSON	The headmaster: Mr. _____
29.	KEY	Used to open Omri's great-grandmother's jewel box
30.	KNIGHT	Source of the battle-ax
31.	KNOT	Cowboy escapes from the dress-up crate through this
32.	LONGHOUSE	Iroquois house
33.	NATIONS	Iroquois Indians were sometimes called this: The Five _____.
34.	PATRICK	Omri's friend
35.	PENICILLIN	Not yet discovered in Tommy's time.
36.	PICTURES	Little Bear criticized Omri's tepee because it lacked these.
37.	PLASTIC	Type of toys that become real in the cupboard.
38.	RAT	It was nesting in the floor under Omri's bed.
39.	SCALPS	Little Bear took thirty of these.
40.	SEED	Little Bear builds his longhouse in the _____ tray.
41.	SHORTS	What Adiel accuses Omri of stealing.
42.	SHOTS	This wakes Omri up at dawn.
43.	SISTERS	Maize, beans, and squash: 3 _____
44.	SKATEBOARD	Omri's birthday gift from his parents
45.	SOLDIER	He believed Omri was a character in a dream.
46.	SPIT	Little Bear cooks on this made from an erector set.
47.	STARS	Little Bear's wife: Bright _____

Copyrighted

Indian In The Cupboard Word List

No.	Word	Clue/Definition
48.	STEALING	Mr. Yapp accused Omri of this.
49.	TEPEE	Where Little Bear sleeps his first night alive
50.	TOMMY	First World War soldier
51.	TRAIL	Book Omri reads about Indians: On the _____ of the Iroquois
52.	TRUTH	What Patrick tells Mr. Johnson
53.	WIFE	If Omri got him this, Little Bear would dance.
54.	YAPP	Owner of the store where Omri purchased plastic figures

Indian In The Cupboard Fill In The Blanks 1

_____ 1. Mr. Yapp accused Omri of this.

_____ 2. Type of toys that become real in the cupboard.

_____ 3. Place where toys come to life

_____ 4. Little Bear's wife: Bright ____

_____ 5. Owner of the store where Omri purchased plastic figures

_____ 6. Indian in the cupboard: Little ____

_____ 7. Boone's best subject in school

_____ 8. Used as a wash basin for Boone & Little Bear: _____ cup

_____ 9. Little Bear removes this from Boone's chest.

_____ 10. What Omri needs from the medical orderly

_____ 11. What Patrick tells Mr. Johnson

_____ 12. Drink Omri gave the Indian

_____ 13. Source of the battle-ax

_____ 14. Cowboy escapes from the dress-up crate through this

_____ 15. It was nesting in the floor under Omri's bed.

_____ 16. Slang for

_____ 17. Omri gave Little Bear canned _____ for breakfast.

_____ 18. Little Bear destroys this

_____ 19. Little Bear criticized Omri's tepee because it lacked these.

_____ 20. Plastic cowboy who comes to life

Indian In The Cupboard Fill In The Blanks 1 Answer Key

STEALING	1. Mr. Yapp accused Omri of this.
PLASTIC	2. Type of toys that become real in the cupboard.
CUPBOARD	3. Place where toys come to life
STARS	4. Little Bear's wife: Bright ____
YAPP	5. Owner of the store where Omri purchased plastic figures
BEAR	6. Indian in the cupboard: Little ____
ART	7. Boone's best subject in school
EGG	8. Used as a wash basin for Boone & Little Bear: ____ cup
ARROW	9. Little Bear removes this from Boone's chest.
BANDAGE	10. What Omri needs from the medical orderly
TRUTH	11. What Patrick tells Mr. Johnson
COKE	12. Drink Omri gave the Indian
KNIGHT	13. Source of the battle-ax
KNOT	14. Cowboy escapes from the dress-up crate through this
RAT	15. It was nesting in the floor under Omri's bed.
BEARD	16. Slang for
BEEF	17. Omri gave Little Bear canned ____ for breakfast.
HEADDRESS	18. Little Bear destroys this
PICTURES	19. Little Bear criticized Omri's tepee because it lacked these.
BOONE	20. Plastic cowboy who comes to life

Indian In The Cupboard Fill In The Blanks 2

_____ 1. Used as a wash basin for Boone & Little Bear: _____ cup

_____ 2. Little Bear took thirty of these.

_____ 3. Drink Omri gave the Indian

_____ 4. Patrick's birthday gift to Omri: Plastic _____

_____ 5. Boone's nickname

_____ 6. It was the size of a football to Little Bear and Boone.

_____ 7. If Omri got him this, Little Bear would dance.

_____ 8. Omri's brother with the missing football shorts

_____ 9. Place where toys come to life

_____ 10. He died inside the cupboard: Indian _____.

_____ 11. What Adiel accuses Omri of stealing.

_____ 12. Little Bear's wife: Bright ____

_____ 13. Book Omri reads about Indians: On the _____ of the Iroquois

_____ 14. The soldier thinks Omri is a _____.

_____ 15. Little Bear belonged to this tribe.

_____ 16. Iroquois house

_____ 17. Reason for Boone's nickname

_____ 18. Maize, beans, and squash: 3 _____

_____ 19. Plastic cowboy who comes to life

_____ 20. Little Bear removes this from Boone's chest.

Indian In The Cupboard Fill In The Blanks 2 Answer Key

EGG	1. Used as a wash basin for Boone & Little Bear: _____ cup
SCALPS	2. Little Bear took thirty of these.
COKE	3. Drink Omri gave the Indian
INDIAN	4. Patrick's birthday gift to Omri: Plastic _____
BOOHOO	5. Boone's nickname
HAIL	6. It was the size of a football to Little Bear and Boone.
WIFE	7. If Omri got him this, Little Bear would dance.
ADIEL	8. Omri's brother with the missing football shorts
CUPBOARD	9. Place where toys come to life
CHIEF	10. He died inside the cupboard: Indian _____.
SHORTS	11. What Adiel accuses Omri of stealing.
STARS	12. Little Bear's wife: Bright _____
TRAIL	13. Book Omri reads about Indians: On the _____ of the Iroquois
DREAM	14. The soldier thinks Omri is a _____.
IROQUOIS	15. Little Bear belonged to this tribe.
LONGHOUSE	16. Iroquois house
CRIES	17. Reason for Boone's nickname
SISTERS	18. Maize, beans, and squash: 3 _____
BOONE	19. Plastic cowboy who comes to life
ARROW	20. Little Bear removes this from Boone's chest.

Indian In The Cupboard Fill In The Blanks 3

_____ 1. Belonged to the dead Indian chief

_____ 2. Little Bear destroys this

_____ 3. Little Bear's wife: Bright ____

_____ 4. It was nesting in the floor under Omri's bed.

_____ 5. Little Bear removes this from Boone's chest.

_____ 6. The soldier thinks Omri is a _____.

_____ 7. Girl who teases Patrick at school

_____ 8. This wakes Omri up at dawn.

_____ 9. He believed Omri was a character in a dream.

_____ 10. Mr. Yapp accused Omri of this.

_____ 11. The headmaster: Mr. _____

_____ 12. Slang for

_____ 13. Omri's birthday gift from his parents

_____ 14. If Omri got him this, Little Bear would dance.

_____ 15. He died inside the cupboard: Indian _____.

_____ 16. Little Bear and Omri; Little Bear and Boone are _____ Brothers

_____ 17. Plastic cowboy who comes to life

_____ 18. Little Bear cooks on this made from an erector set.

_____ 19. Maize, beans, and squash: 3 _____

_____ 20. Place where toys come to life

Indian In The Cupboard Fill In The Blanks 3 Answer Key

BOW	1. Belonged to the dead Indian chief
HEADDRESS	2. Little Bear destroys this
STARS	3. Little Bear's wife: Bright ____
RAT	4. It was nesting in the floor under Omri's bed.
ARROW	5. Little Bear removes this from Boone's chest.
DREAM	6. The soldier thinks Omri is a ____.
APRIL	7. Girl who teases Patrick at school
SHOTS	8. This wakes Omri up at dawn.
SOLDIER	9. He believed Omri was a character in a dream.
STEALING	10. Mr. Yapp accused Omri of this.
JOHNSON	11. The headmaster: Mr. ____
BEARD	12. Slang for
SKATEBOARD	13. Omri's birthday gift from his parents
WIFE	14. If Omri got him this, Little Bear would dance.
CHIEF	15. He died inside the cupboard: Indian ____.
BLOOD	16. Little Bear and Omri; Little Bear and Boone are ____ Brothers
BOONE	17. Plastic cowboy who comes to life
SPIT	18. Little Bear cooks on this made from an erector set.
SISTERS	19. Maize, beans, and squash: 3 ____
CUPBOARD	20. Place where toys come to life

Indian In The Cupboard Fill In The Blanks 4

_____ 1. Used to open Omri's great-grandmother's jewel box

_____ 2. Maize, beans, and squash: 3 _____

_____ 3. What Patrick tells Mr. Johnson

_____ 4. Little Bear gave Omri this as payment for his wife.

_____ 5. Boone's nickname

_____ 6. First World War soldier

_____ 7. Little Bear removes this from Boone's chest.

_____ 8. Iroquois Indians were sometimes called this: The Five _____.

_____ 9. Indian in the cupboard: Little ____

_____ 10. Type of toys that become real in the cupboard.

_____ 11. Source of the battle-ax

_____ 12. Used as a wash basin for Boone & Little Bear: _____ cup

_____ 13. Boone's best subject in school

_____ 14. Little Bear builds his longhouse in the _____ tray.

_____ 15. Drink Omri gave the Indian

_____ 16. Where Little Bear sleeps his first night alive

_____ 17. Little Bear cooks on this made from an erector set.

_____ 18. Slang for

_____ 19. Girl who teases Patrick at school

_____ 20. Omri's brother who gave Omri the cupboard

Indian In The Cupboard Fill In The Blanks 4 Answer Key

KEY	1. Used to open Omri's great-grandmother's jewel box
SISTERS	2. Maize, beans, and squash: 3 _____
TRUTH	3. What Patrick tells Mr. Johnson
BELT	4. Little Bear gave Omri this as payment for his wife.
BOOHOO	5. Boone's nickname
TOMMY	6. First World War soldier
ARROW	7. Little Bear removes this from Boone's chest.
NATIONS	8. Iroquois Indians were sometimes called this: The Five _____.
BEAR	9. Indian in the cupboard: Little ____
PLASTIC	10. Type of toys that become real in the cupboard.
KNIGHT	11. Source of the battle-ax
EGG	12. Used as a wash basin for Boone & Little Bear: _____ cup
ART	13. Boone's best subject in school
SEED	14. Little Bear builds his longhouse in the _____ tray.
COKE	15. Drink Omri gave the Indian
TEPEE	16. Where Little Bear sleeps his first night alive
SPIT	17. Little Bear cooks on this made from an erector set.
BEARD	18. Slang for
APRIL	19. Girl who teases Patrick at school
GILLON	20. Omri's brother who gave Omri the cupboard

Indian In The Cupboard Matching 1

___ 1. SCALPS   A. Little Bear removes this from Boone's chest.
___ 2. KNOT   B. Type of toys that become real in the cupboard.
___ 3. JOHNSON   C. Reason for Boone's nickname
___ 4. SHOTS   D. Cowboy escapes from the dress-up crate through this
___ 5. SISTERS   E. Where Little Bear sleeps his first night alive
___ 6. SPIT   F. This wakes Omri up at dawn.
___ 7. CHIEF   G. Maize, beans, and squash: 3 _____
___ 8. BEAR   H. Boone's best subject in school
___ 9. HEADDRESS   I. Little Bear took thirty of these.
___10. HAIL   J. Mr. Yapp accused Omri of this.
___11. TEPEE   K. Girl who teases Patrick at school
___12. CRIES   L. He died inside the cupboard: Indian _____.
___13. ARROW   M. Not yet discovered in Tommy's time.
___14. ADIEL   N. It was the size of a football to Little Bear and Boone.
___15. LONGHOUSE   O. Iroquois house
___16. BEEF   P. Little Bear destroys this
___17. COKE   Q. Omri gave Little Bear canned _____ for breakfast.
___18. ART   R. Omri's friend
___19. STEALING   S. Boone's nickname for Omri: _____-Nation
___20. PATRICK   T. The headmaster: Mr. _____
___21. HALLUCY   U. Omri's brother with the missing football shorts
___22. PLASTIC   V. Drink Omri gave the Indian
___23. BOONE   W. Indian in the cupboard: Little ____
___24. PENICILLIN   X. Little Bear cooks on this made from an erector set.
___25. APRIL   Y. Plastic cowboy who comes to life

Indian In The Cupboard Matching 1 Answer Key

I - 1.	SCALPS	A. Little Bear removes this from Boone's chest.
D - 2.	KNOT	B. Type of toys that become real in the cupboard.
T - 3.	JOHNSON	C. Reason for Boone's nickname
F - 4.	SHOTS	D. Cowboy escapes from the dress-up crate through this
G - 5.	SISTERS	E. Where Little Bear sleeps his first night alive
X - 6.	SPIT	F. This wakes Omri up at dawn.
L - 7.	CHIEF	G. Maize, beans, and squash: 3 _____
W - 8.	BEAR	H. Boone's best subject in school
P - 9.	HEADDRESS	I. Little Bear took thirty of these.
N -10.	HAIL	J. Mr. Yapp accused Omri of this.
E -11.	TEPEE	K. Girl who teases Patrick at school
C -12.	CRIES	L. He died inside the cupboard: Indian _____.
A -13.	ARROW	M. Not yet discovered in Tommy's time.
U -14.	ADIEL	N. It was the size of a football to Little Bear and Boone.
O -15.	LONGHOUSE	O. Iroquois house
Q -16.	BEEF	P. Little Bear destroys this
V -17.	COKE	Q. Omri gave Little Bear canned _____ for breakfast.
H -18.	ART	R. Omri's friend
J -19.	STEALING	S. Boone's nickname for Omri: _____-Nation
R -20.	PATRICK	T. The headmaster: Mr. _____
S -21.	HALLUCY	U. Omri's brother with the missing football shorts
B -22.	PLASTIC	V. Drink Omri gave the Indian
Y -23.	BOONE	W. Indian in the cupboard: Little ____
M -24.	PENICILLIN	X. Little Bear cooks on this made from an erector set.
K -25.	APRIL	Y. Plastic cowboy who comes to life

Indian In The Cupboard Matching 2

___ 1. WIFE A. This wakes Omri up at dawn.
___ 2. PENICILLIN B. Plastic cowboy who comes to life
___ 3. SEED C. If Omri got him this, Little Bear would dance.
___ 4. RAT D. Little Bear gave Omri this as payment for his wife.
___ 5. BELT E. Owner of the store where Omri purchased plastic figures
___ 6. DREAM F. What Patrick tells Mr. Johnson
___ 7. PATRICK G. Not yet discovered in Tommy's time.
___ 8. BOONE H. Place where toys come to life
___ 9. KNOT I. Omri's friend
___10. PLASTIC J. Boone's best subject in school
___11. KNIGHT K. Omri's birthday gift from his parents
___12. SOLDIER L. Type of toys that become real in the cupboard.
___13. SHOTS M. Source of the battle-ax
___14. STARS N. First World War soldier
___15. CUPBOARD O. Little Bear's wife: Bright _____
___16. SKATEBOARD P. Little Bear builds his longhouse in the _____ tray.
___17. BOOHOO Q. Boone's nickname for Omri:_____-Nation
___18. ART R. Cowboy escapes from the dress-up crate through this
___19. LONGHOUSE S. Used as a wash basin for Boone & Little Bear: _____ cup
___20. NATIONS T. Iroquois house
___21. TRUTH U. He believed Omri was a character in a dream.
___22. EGG V. Iroquois Indians were sometimes called this: The Five _____.
___23. YAPP W. It was nesting in the floor under Omri's bed.
___24. HALLUCY X. Boone's nickname
___25. TOMMY Y. The soldier thinks Omri is a _____.

Indian In The Cupboard Matching 2 Answer Key

C - 1. WIFE	A. This wakes Omri up at dawn.
G - 2. PENICILLIN	B. Plastic cowboy who comes to life
P - 3. SEED	C. If Omri got him this, Little Bear would dance.
W - 4. RAT	D. Little Bear gave Omri this as payment for his wife.
D - 5. BELT	E. Owner of the store where Omri purchased plastic figures
Y - 6. DREAM	F. What Patrick tells Mr. Johnson
I - 7. PATRICK	G. Not yet discovered in Tommy's time.
B - 8. BOONE	H. Place where toys come to life
R - 9. KNOT	I. Omri's friend
L - 10. PLASTIC	J. Boone's best subject in school
M - 11. KNIGHT	K. Omri's birthday gift from his parents
U - 12. SOLDIER	L. Type of toys that become real in the cupboard.
A - 13. SHOTS	M. Source of the battle-ax
O - 14. STARS	N. First World War soldier
H - 15. CUPBOARD	O. Little Bear's wife: Bright _____
K - 16. SKATEBOARD	P. Little Bear builds his longhouse in the _____ tray.
X - 17. BOOHOO	Q. Boone's nickname for Omri: _____-Nation
J - 18. ART	R. Cowboy escapes from the dress-up crate through this
T - 19. LONGHOUSE	S. Used as a wash basin for Boone & Little Bear: _____ cup
V - 20. NATIONS	T. Iroquois house
F - 21. TRUTH	U. He believed Omri was a character in a dream.
S - 22. EGG	V. Iroquois Indians were sometimes called this: The Five _____.
E - 23. YAPP	W. It was nesting in the floor under Omri's bed.
Q - 24. HALLUCY	X. Boone's nickname
N - 25. TOMMY	Y. The soldier thinks Omri is a _____.

Indian In The Cupboard Matching 3

___ 1. SKATEBOARD		A. Omri gave Little Bear canned _____ for breakfast.
___ 2. TEPEE			B. First World War soldier
___ 3. ADIEL			C. Maize, beans, and squash: 3 _____
___ 4. PENICILLIN		D. Reason for Boone's nickname
___ 5. WIFE			E. Boone's best subject in school
___ 6. KNOT			F. Omri's mother plans to keep the key on this
___ 7. ART			G. Not yet discovered in Tommy's time.
___ 8. BOOHOO		H. Source of the battle-ax
___ 9. CHAIN			I. Mr. Yapp accused Omri of this.
___ 10. YAPP			J. Little Bear destroys this
___ 11. CRIES			K. Little Bear took thirty of these.
___ 12. SISTERS		L. Owner of the store where Omri purchased plastic figures
___ 13. BOW			M. Patrick's birthday gift to Omri: Plastic _____
___ 14. BELT			N. Girl who teases Patrick at school
___ 15. KNIGHT		O. Omri's brother with the missing football shorts
___ 16. INDIAN		P. He died inside the cupboard: Indian _____.
___ 17. CHIEF			Q. Where Little Bear sleeps his first night alive
___ 18. CUPBOARD		R. Cowboy escapes from the dress-up crate through this
___ 19. JOHNSON		S. Belonged to the dead Indian chief
___ 20. SCALPS		T. Little Bear gave Omri this as payment for his wife.
___ 21. TOMMY		U. The headmaster: Mr. _____
___ 22. STEALING		V. Omri's birthday gift from his parents
___ 23. HEADDRESS	W. Boone's nickname
___ 24. APRIL			X. Place where toys come to life
___ 25. BEEF			Y. If Omri got him this, Little Bear would dance.

Indian In The Cupboard Matching 3 Answer Key

V - 1. SKATEBOARD		A. Omri gave Little Bear canned _____ for breakfast.
Q - 2. TEPEE		B. First World War soldier
O - 3. ADIEL		C. Maize, beans, and squash: 3 _____
G - 4. PENICILLIN		D. Reason for Boone's nickname
Y - 5. WIFE		E. Boone's best subject in school
R - 6. KNOT		F. Omri's mother plans to keep the key on this
E - 7. ART		G. Not yet discovered in Tommy's time.
W - 8. BOOHOO		H. Source of the battle-ax
F - 9. CHAIN		I. Mr. Yapp accused Omri of this.
L - 10. YAPP		J. Little Bear destroys this
D - 11. CRIES		K. Little Bear took thirty of these.
C - 12. SISTERS		L. Owner of the store where Omri purchased plastic figures
S - 13. BOW		M. Patrick's birthday gift to Omri: Plastic _____
T - 14. BELT		N. Girl who teases Patrick at school
H - 15. KNIGHT		O. Omri's brother with the missing football shorts
M - 16. INDIAN		P. He died inside the cupboard: Indian _____.
P - 17. CHIEF		Q. Where Little Bear sleeps his first night alive
X - 18. CUPBOARD		R. Cowboy escapes from the dress-up crate through this
U - 19. JOHNSON		S. Belonged to the dead Indian chief
K - 20. SCALPS		T. Little Bear gave Omri this as payment for his wife.
B - 21. TOMMY		U. The headmaster: Mr. _____
I - 22. STEALING		V. Omri's birthday gift from his parents
J - 23. HEADDRESS		W. Boone's nickname
N - 24. APRIL		X. Place where toys come to life
A - 25. BEEF		Y. If Omri got him this, Little Bear would dance.

Indian In The Cupboard Matching 4

___ 1. TOMMY   A. If Omri got him this, Little Bear would dance.
___ 2. ART   B. Where Little Bear sleeps his first night alive
___ 3. CUPBOARD   C. Place where toys come to life
___ 4. PLASTIC   D. Type of toys that become real in the cupboard.
___ 5. TRUTH   E. Cowboy escapes from the dress-up crate through this
___ 6. TEPEE   F. Little Bear belonged to this tribe.
___ 7. SEED   G. It was nesting in the floor under Omri's bed.
___ 8. HAIL   H. What Adiel accuses Omri of stealing.
___ 9. BANDAGE   I. Used to open Omri's great-grandmother's jewel box
___ 10. HALLUCY   J. What Omri needs from the medical orderly
___ 11. YAPP   K. First World War soldier
___ 12. BEEF   L. Owner of the store where Omri purchased plastic figures
___ 13. HEADDRESS   M. Little Bear destroys this
___ 14. TRAIL   N. Book Omri reads about Indians: On the _____ of the Iroquois
___ 15. KNOT   O. Boone's best subject in school
___ 16. RAT   P. Omri's friend
___ 17. PATRICK   Q. Iroquois Indians were sometimes called this: The Five _____.
___ 18. BEARD   R. Girl who teases Patrick at school
___ 19. NATIONS   S. What Patrick tells Mr. Johnson
___ 20. IROQUOIS   T. Little Bear builds his longhouse in the _____ tray.
___ 21. APRIL   U. It was the size of a football to Little Bear and Boone.
___ 22. GILLON   V. Omri's brother who gave Omri the cupboard
___ 23. SHORTS   W. Omri gave Little Bear canned _____ for breakfast.
___ 24. WIFE   X. Slang for
___ 25. KEY   Y. Boone's nickname for Omri: _____-Nation

Indian In The Cupboard Matching 4 Answer Key

K - 1.	TOMMY	A.	If Omri got him this, Little Bear would dance.
O - 2.	ART	B.	Where Little Bear sleeps his first night alive
C - 3.	CUPBOARD	C.	Place where toys come to life
D - 4.	PLASTIC	D.	Type of toys that become real in the cupboard.
S - 5.	TRUTH	E.	Cowboy escapes from the dress-up crate through this
B - 6.	TEPEE	F.	Little Bear belonged to this tribe.
T - 7.	SEED	G.	It was nesting in the floor under Omri's bed.
U - 8.	HAIL	H.	What Adiel accuses Omri of stealing.
J - 9.	BANDAGE	I.	Used to open Omri's great-grandmother's jewel box
Y -10.	HALLUCY	J.	What Omri needs from the medical orderly
L -11.	YAPP	K.	First World War soldier
W -12.	BEEF	L.	Owner of the store where Omri purchased plastic figures
M -13.	HEADDRESS	M.	Little Bear destroys this
N -14.	TRAIL	N.	Book Omri reads about Indians: On the _____ of the Iroquois
E -15.	KNOT	O.	Boone's best subject in school
G -16.	RAT	P.	Omri's friend
P -17.	PATRICK	Q.	Iroquois Indians were sometimes called this: The Five _____.
X -18.	BEARD	R.	Girl who teases Patrick at school
Q -19.	NATIONS	S.	What Patrick tells Mr. Johnson
F -20.	IROQUOIS	T.	Little Bear builds his longhouse in the _____ tray.
R -21.	APRIL	U.	It was the size of a football to Little Bear and Boone.
V -22.	GILLON	V.	Omri's brother who gave Omri the cupboard
H -23.	SHORTS	W.	Omri gave Little Bear canned _____ for breakfast.
A -24.	WIFE	X.	Slang for
I - 25.	KEY	Y.	Boone's nickname for Omri:_____-Nation

Indian In The Cupboard Magic Squares 1

Match the definition with the vocabulary word. Put your answers in the magic squares below. When your answers are correct, all columns and rows will add to the same number.

A. SISTERS
B. SPIT
C. PENICILLIN
D. BOONE
E. CHAIN
F. SHORTS
G. STEALING
H. COKE
I. CRIES
J. GILLON
K. COWBOY
L. BOOHOO
M. STARS
N. TEPEE
O. ART
P. PICTURES

1. Where Little Bear sleeps his first night alive
2. Mr. Yapp accused Omri of this.
3. Boone's nickname
4. Maize, beans, and squash: 3 _____
5. Omri was afraid Little Bear would kill him.
6. Little Bear cooks on this made from an erector set.
7. Little Bear's wife: Bright ____
8. Drink Omri gave the Indian
9. Omri's mother plans to keep the key on this
10. Little Bear criticized Omri's tepee because it lacked these.
11. Not yet discovered in Tommy's time.
12. Omri's brother who gave Omri the cupboard
13. Plastic cowboy who comes to life
14. Reason for Boone's nickname
15. What Adiel accuses Omri of stealing.
16. Boone's best subject in school

A=	B=	C=	D=
E=	F=	G=	H=
I=	J=	K=	L=
M=	N=	O=	P=

Indian In The Cupboard Magic Squares 1 Answer Key

Match the definition with the vocabulary word. Put your answers in the magic squares below. When your answers are correct, all columns and rows will add to the same number.

A. SISTERS
B. SPIT
C. PENICILLIN
D. BOONE
E. CHAIN
F. SHORTS
G. STEALING
H. COKE
I. CRIES
J. GILLON
K. COWBOY
L. BOOHOO
M. STARS
N. TEPEE
O. ART
P. PICTURES

1. Where Little Bear sleeps his first night alive
2. Mr. Yapp accused Omri of this.
3. Boone's nickname
4. Maize, beans, and squash: 3 _____
5. Omri was afraid Little Bear would kill him.
6. Little Bear cooks on this made from an erector set.
7. Little Bear's wife: Bright ____
8. Drink Omri gave the Indian
9. Omri's mother plans to keep the key on this
10. Little Bear criticized Omri's tepee because it lacked these.
11. Not yet discovered in Tommy's time.
12. Omri's brother who gave Omri the cupboard
13. Plastic cowboy who comes to life
14. Reason for Boone's nickname
15. What Adiel accuses Omri of stealing.
16. Boone's best subject in school

A=4	B=6	C=11	D=13
E=9	F=15	G=2	H=8
I=14	J=12	K=5	L=3
M=7	N=1	O=16	P=10

Indian In The Cupboard Magic Squares 2

Match the definition with the vocabulary word. Put your answers in the magic squares below. When your answers are correct, all columns and rows will add to the same number.

A. BEAR
B. BEARD
C. PENICILLIN
D. ARROW
E. HALLUCY
F. TEPEE
G. EGG
H. SISTERS
I. TOMMY
J. SHOTS
K. SOLDIER
L. ART
M. DREAM
N. LONGHOUSE
O. PATRICK
P. BOW

1. The soldier thinks Omri is a _____.
2. Where Little Bear sleeps his first night alive
3. Maize, beans, and squash: 3 _____
4. Omri's friend
5. Boone's best subject in school
6. Not yet discovered in Tommy's time.
7. Indian in the cupboard: Little _____
8. This wakes Omri up at dawn.
9. He believed Omri was a character in a dream.
10. Little Bear removes this from Boone's chest.
11. Slang for
12. First World War soldier
13. Iroquois house
14. Boone's nickname for Omri:_____-Nation
15. Used as a wash basin for Boone & Little Bear: _____ cup
16. Belonged to the dead Indian chief

A=	B=	C=	D=
E=	F=	G=	H=
I=	J=	K=	L=
M=	N=	O=	P=

Indian In The Cupboard Magic Squares 2 Answer Key

Match the definition with the vocabulary word. Put your answers in the magic squares below. When your answers are correct, all columns and rows will add to the same number.

A. BEAR
B. BEARD
C. PENICILLIN
D. ARROW
E. HALLUCY
F. TEPEE
G. EGG
H. SISTERS
I. TOMMY
J. SHOTS
K. SOLDIER
L. ART
M. DREAM
N. LONGHOUSE
O. PATRICK
P. BOW

1. The soldier thinks Omri is a _____.
2. Where Little Bear sleeps his first night alive
3. Maize, beans, and squash: 3 _____
4. Omri's friend
5. Boone's best subject in school
6. Not yet discovered in Tommy's time.
7. Indian in the cupboard: Little ____
8. This wakes Omri up at dawn.
9. He believed Omri was a character in a dream.
10. Little Bear removes this from Boone's chest.
11. Slang for
12. First World War soldier
13. Iroquois house
14. Boone's nickname for Omri:_____-Nation
15. Used as a wash basin for Boone & Little Bear: _____ cup
16. Belonged to the dead Indian chief

A=7	B=11	C=6	D=10
E=14	F=2	G=15	H=3
I=12	J=8	K=9	L=5
M=1	N=13	O=4	P=16

Indian In The Cupboard Magic Squares 3

Match the definition with the vocabulary word. Put your answers in the magic squares below. When your answers are correct, all columns and rows will add to the same number.

A. CRIES
B. PLASTIC
C. COWBOY
D. LONGHOUSE
E. BANDAGE
F. SCALPS
G. BOONE
H. CHIEF
I. KEY
J. GILLON
K. PENICILLIN
L. HAIL
M. COKE
N. JOHNSON
O. TEPEE
P. NATIONS

1. Omri was afraid Little Bear would kill him.
2. Omri's brother who gave Omri the cupboard
3. Little Bear took thirty of these.
4. Where Little Bear sleeps his first night alive
5. Iroquois Indians were sometimes called this: The Five _____.
6. What Omri needs from the medical orderly
7. Used to open Omri's great-grandmother's jewel box
8. Iroquois house
9. Drink Omri gave the Indian
10. He died inside the cupboard: Indian _____.
11. It was the size of a football to Little Bear and Boone.
12. Reason for Boone's nickname
13. Type of toys that become real in the cupboard.
14. Not yet discovered in Tommy's time.
15. Plastic cowboy who comes to life
16. The headmaster: Mr. _____

A=	B=	C=	D=
E=	F=	G=	H=
I=	J=	K=	L=
M=	N=	O=	P=

Indian In The Cupboard Magic Squares 3 Answer Key

Match the definition with the vocabulary word. Put your answers in the magic squares below. When your answers are correct, all columns and rows will add to the same number.

A. CRIES
B. PLASTIC
C. COWBOY
D. LONGHOUSE
E. BANDAGE
F. SCALPS
G. BOONE
H. CHIEF
I. KEY
J. GILLON
K. PENICILLIN
L. HAIL
M. COKE
N. JOHNSON
O. TEPEE
P. NATIONS

1. Omri was afraid Little Bear would kill him.
2. Omri's brother who gave Omri the cupboard
3. Little Bear took thirty of these.
4. Where Little Bear sleeps his first night alive
5. Iroquois Indians were sometimes called this: The Five _____.
6. What Omri needs from the medical orderly
7. Used to open Omri's great-grandmother's jewel box
8. Iroquois house
9. Drink Omri gave the Indian
10. He died inside the cupboard: Indian _____.
11. It was the size of a football to Little Bear and Boone.
12. Reason for Boone's nickname
13. Type of toys that become real in the cupboard.
14. Not yet discovered in Tommy's time.
15. Plastic cowboy who comes to life
16. The headmaster: Mr. _____

A=12	B=13	C=1	D=8
E=6	F=3	G=15	H=10
I=7	J=2	K=14	L=11
M=9	N=16	O=4	P=5

Indian In The Cupboard Magic Squares 4

Match the definition with the vocabulary word. Put your answers in the magic squares below. When your answers are correct, all columns and rows will add to the same number.

A. BLOOD
B. BEARD
C. PATRICK
D. RAT

E. NATIONS
F. KEY
G. DREAM
H. STARS

I. YAPP
J. ART
K. BOONE
L. BEAR

M. BOOHOO
N. HEADDRESS
O. LONGHOUSE
P. CUPBOARD

1. Little Bear and Omri; Little Bear and Boone are _____ Brothers
2. Little Bear destroys this
3. Boone's best subject in school
4. Iroquois Indians were sometimes called this: The Five _____.
5. The soldier thinks Omri is a _____.
6. Indian in the cupboard: Little _____
7. Place where toys come to life
8. Omri's friend
9. Iroquois house
10. It was nesting in the floor under Omri's bed.
11. Little Bear's wife: Bright _____
12. Plastic cowboy who comes to life
13. Owner of the store where Omri purchased plastic figures
14. Used to open Omri's great-grandmother's jewel box
15. Slang for
16. Boone's nickname

A=	B=	C=	D=
E=	F=	G=	H=
I=	J=	K=	L=
M=	N=	O=	P=

Indian In The Cupboard Magic Squares 4 Answer Key

Match the definition with the vocabulary word. Put your answers in the magic squares below. When your answers are correct, all columns and rows will add to the same number.

A. BLOOD
B. BEARD
C. PATRICK
D. RAT
E. NATIONS
F. KEY
G. DREAM
H. STARS
I. YAPP
J. ART
K. BOONE
L. BEAR
M. BOOHOO
N. HEADDRESS
O. LONGHOUSE
P. CUPBOARD

1. Little Bear and Omri; Little Bear and Boone are _____ Brothers
2. Little Bear destroys this
3. Boone's best subject in school
4. Iroquois Indians were sometimes called this: The Five _____.
5. The soldier thinks Omri is a _____.
6. Indian in the cupboard: Little _____
7. Place where toys come to life
8. Omri's friend
9. Iroquois house
10. It was nesting in the floor under Omri's bed.
11. Little Bear's wife: Bright _____
12. Plastic cowboy who comes to life
13. Owner of the store where Omri purchased plastic figures
14. Used to open Omri's great-grandmother's jewel box
15. Slang for
16. Boone's nickname

A=1	B=15	C=8	D=10
E=4	F=14	G=5	H=11
I=13	J=3	K=12	L=6
M=16	N=2	O=9	P=7

Indian In The Cupboard Word Search 1

```
A R T R Q Q B J Y S S E R D D A E H S
N R A G D C E L Y I C P P B N C A B H
L E R H V F L L O Z M Y I V L P N B O
B J B O Q M T U S O H A T L T A N R
P O O M W M Q S C Y D H W U S O T D T
E H O G S O T A A C J C R T M R A S
N N H C R F H E L P K Y E X A M I G D
I S O I E G G A P P K T F X R Y C E R
C O O E B I I L S E S L H R S D K X H
I N B Z W L N I L I E D X E R M M T P
L N V F D L K N S I G X K E Q G U C W
W A S W O E G D Y X O I Q B R P Z J
I B P T B N F A O K C D G D T E H H S
N O R S I O I B C N L S S R Y G A E J
L O I C F O W S H O T S A E Z G I R P
R N L M L O N X S T K I K A E R L A D
F E I H C Y M S G N L T N M C D L T X
```

Belonged to the dead Indian chief (3)
Book Omri reads about Indians: On the _____ of the Iroquois (5)
Boone's best subject in school (3)
Boone's nickname (6)
Boone's nickname for Omri:_____-Nation (7)
Cowboy escapes from the dress-up crate through this (4)
Drink Omri gave the Indian (4)
First World War soldier (5)
Girl who teases Patrick at school (5)
He believed Omri was a character in a dream. (7)
He died inside the cupboard: Indian _____. (5)
If Omri got him this, Little Bear would dance. (4)
Indian in the cupboard: Little _____ (4)
Iroquois Indians were sometimes called this: The Five _____. (7)
It was nesting in the floor under Omri's bed. (3)
It was the size of a football to Little Bear and Boone. (4)
Little Bear and Omri; Little Bear and Boone are _____ Brothers (5)
Little Bear belonged to this tribe. (8)
Little Bear builds his longhouse in the _____ tray. (4)
Little Bear cooks on this made from an erector set. (4)
Little Bear destroys this (9)
Little Bear gave Omri this as payment for his wife. (4)
Little Bear removes this from Boone's chest. (5)

Little Bear took thirty of these. (6)
Little Bear's wife: Bright _____ (5)
Maize, beans, and squash: 3 _____ (7)
Mr. Yapp accused Omri of this. (8)
Not yet discovered in Tommy's time. (10)
Omri gave Little Bear canned _____ for breakfast. (4)
Omri was afraid Little Bear would kill him. (6)
Omri's brother who gave Omri the cupboard (6)
Omri's brother with the missing football shorts (5)
Omri's friend (7)
Omri's mother plans to keep the key on this (5)
Owner of the store where Omri purchased plastic figures (4)
Plastic cowboy who comes to life (5)
Reason for Boone's nickname (5)
Slang for (5)
Source of the battle-ax (6)
The headmaster: Mr. _____ (7)
The soldier thinks Omri is a _____. (5)
This wakes Omri up at dawn. (5)
Used as a wash basin for Boone & Little Bear: _____ cup (3)
Used to open Omri's great-grandmother's jewel box (3)
What Adiel accuses Omri of stealing. (6)
What Omri needs from the medical orderly (7)
What Patrick tells Mr. Johnson (5)
Where Little Bear sleeps his first night alive (5)

Indian In The Cupboard Word Search 1 Answer Key

Belonged to the dead Indian chief (3)
Book Omri reads about Indians: On the _____ of the Iroquois (5)
Boone's best subject in school (3)
Boone's nickname (6)
Boone's nickname for Omri: _____-Nation (7)
Cowboy escapes from the dress-up crate through this (4)
Drink Omri gave the Indian (4)
First World War soldier (5)
Girl who teases Patrick at school (5)
He believed Omri was a character in a dream. (7)
He died inside the cupboard: Indian _____. (5)
If Omri got him this, Little Bear would dance. (4)
Indian in the cupboard: Little _____ (4)
Iroquois Indians were sometimes called this: The Five _____. (7)
It was nesting in the floor under Omri's bed. (3)
It was the size of a football to Little Bear and Boone. (4)
Little Bear and Omri; Little Bear and Boone are _____ Brothers (5)
Little Bear belonged to this tribe. (8)
Little Bear builds his longhouse in the _____ tray. (4)
Little Bear cooks on this made from an erector set. (4)
Little Bear destroys this (9)
Little Bear gave Omri this as payment for his wife. (4)
Little Bear removes this from Boone's chest. (5)
Little Bear took thirty of these. (6)
Little Bear's wife: Bright _____ (5)
Maize, beans, and squash: 3 _____ (7)
Mr. Yapp accused Omri of this. (8)
Not yet discovered in Tommy's time. (10)
Omri gave Little Bear canned _____ for breakfast. (4)
Omri was afraid Little Bear would kill him. (6)
Omri's brother who gave Omri the cupboard (6)
Omri's brother with the missing football shorts (5)
Omri's friend (7)
Omri's mother plans to keep the key on this (5)
Owner of the store where Omri purchased plastic figures (4)
Plastic cowboy who comes to life (5)
Reason for Boone's nickname (5)
Slang for (5)
Source of the battle-ax (6)
The headmaster: Mr. _____ (7)
The soldier thinks Omri is a _____. (5)
This wakes Omri up at dawn. (5)
Used as a wash basin for Boone & Little Bear: _____ cup (3)
Used to open Omri's great-grandmother's jewel box (3)
What Adiel accuses Omri of stealing. (6)
What Omri needs from the medical orderly (7)
What Patrick tells Mr. Johnson (5)
Where Little Bear sleeps his first night alive (5)

Indian In The Cupboard Word Search 2

```
B E A R D B O O H O O Q W F T C J E L
X H P S P L B O N E O E W R W N K J
B A I T A C O A T R I B D A Y T O P
N L C S H B T C R H J X N I G H C X
O L T R H I R A C X R S Z L N W R P
L U E Y O R E I D L O S E S B I Q P
L C R N Z J K G C R S O E W F L R
I Y E S T H G I N K K T N M G D E Y Z
G N S K T G Z L G E R I A G R B M K D
B W D B E A J K Y O A E S A H M N V B
O T H I C Y R X H H R I O K O O R F W
W S P L A C S S C D O B S T T R U T H
V B I E S N P Y M U E L E H Y E A S P
Z A Y I J T T V Q T Z O H E O A P T E
H S V D T Z K O A T R O Z Y F T P E Z
N B E A R W R K R H C D C R I E S P E
A P R I L I S A H E A D D R E S S X V
```

Belonged to the dead Indian chief (3)
Book Omri reads about Indians: On the _____ of the Iroquois (5)
Boone's best subject in school (3)
Boone's nickname (6)
Boone's nickname for Omri: _____-Nation (7)
Cowboy escapes from the dress-up crate through this (4)
Drink Omri gave the Indian (4)
First World War soldier (5)
Girl who teases Patrick at school (5)
He believed Omri was a character in a dream. (7)
He died inside the cupboard: Indian _____. (5)
If Omri got him this, Little Bear would dance. (4)
Indian in the cupboard: Little _____ (4)
Iroquois Indians were sometimes called this: The Five _____. (7)
Iroquois house (9)
It was nesting in the floor under Omri's bed. (3)
It was the size of a football to Little Bear and Boone. (4)
Little Bear and Omri; Little Bear and Boone are _____ Brothers (5)
Little Bear belonged to this tribe. (8)
Little Bear builds his longhouse in the _____ tray. (4)
Little Bear cooks on this made from an erector set. (4)
Little Bear criticized Omri's tepee because it lacked these. (8)
Little Bear destroys this (9)

Little Bear gave Omri this as payment for his wife. (4)
Little Bear removes this from Boone's chest. (5)
Little Bear took thirty of these. (6)
Little Bear's wife: Bright ____ (5)
Maize, beans, and squash: 3 _____ (7)
Omri gave Little Bear canned _____ for breakfast. (4)
Omri's birthday gift from his parents (10)
Omri's brother who gave Omri the cupboard (6)
Omri's brother with the missing football shorts (5)
Omri's friend (7)
Omri's mother plans to keep the key on this (5)
Owner of the store where Omri purchased plastic figures (4)
Patrick's birthday gift to Omri: Plastic _____ (6)
Plastic cowboy who comes to life (5)
Reason for Boone's nickname (5)
Slang for (5)
Source of the battle-ax (6)
The headmaster: Mr. _____ (7)
The soldier thinks Omri is a _____. (5)
This wakes Omri up at dawn. (5)
Used as a wash basin for Boone & Little Bear: _____ cup (3)
Used to open Omri's great-grandmother's jewel box (3)
What Adiel accuses Omri of stealing. (6)
What Patrick tells Mr. Johnson (5)
Where Little Bear sleeps his first night alive (5)

Indian In The Cupboard Word Search 2 Answer Key

```
B E A R D B O O H O O     W F T     E
  H P S P     B O O N E O E R     K J
  A I I   A   A   R   E   A     O
N L C S   T T   R H   S   L N   H C
O L T T   I R A C     S   N   W
L U R R   O R E I D L O S E S     T
L C E R N     C   C   S O E F   L
I Y E S T H G I N K K T N   D E Y
G N S   T G   E R I A G R B M K
B   D   E A   Y O A E S A H M N
O     I     R   H H R I O   O O
W S P L A C S S C D O B S T T R U T H
  A I E   N P   U E L E H Y E A S
  H   D T     O A T   O   F T P E E
      B E A R   R K R     D C R I E S P E
  A P R I L I S A H E A D D R E S S
```

Belonged to the dead Indian chief (3)
Book Omri reads about Indians: On the _____ of the Iroquois (5)
Boone's best subject in school (3)
Boone's nickname (6)
Boone's nickname for Omri:_____-Nation (7)
Cowboy escapes from the dress-up crate through this (4)
Drink Omri gave the Indian (4)
First World War soldier (5)
Girl who teases Patrick at school (5)
He believed Omri was a character in a dream. (7)
He died inside the cupboard: Indian _____. (5)
If Omri got him this, Little Bear would dance. (4)
Indian in the cupboard: Little ____ (4)
Iroquois Indians were sometimes called this: The Five _____. (7)
Iroquois house (9)
It was nesting in the floor under Omri's bed. (3)
It was the size of a football to Little Bear and Boone. (4)
Little Bear and Omri; Little Bear and Boone are _____ Brothers (5)
Little Bear belonged to this tribe. (8)
Little Bear builds his longhouse in the _____ tray. (4)
Little Bear cooks on this made from an erector set. (4)
Little Bear criticized Omri's tepee because it lacked these. (8)
Little Bear destroys this (9)

Little Bear gave Omri this as payment for his wife. (4)
Little Bear removes this from Boone's chest. (5)
Little Bear took thirty of these. (6)
Little Bear's wife: Bright ____ (5)
Maize, beans, and squash: 3 _____ (7)
Omri gave Little Bear canned _____ for breakfast. (4)
Omri's birthday gift from his parents (10)
Omri's brother who gave Omri the cupboard (6)
Omri's brother with the missing football shorts (5)
Omri's friend (7)
Omri's mother plans to keep the key on this (5)
Owner of the store where Omri purchased plastic figures (4)
Patrick's birthday gift to Omri: Plastic _____ (6)
Plastic cowboy who comes to life (5)
Reason for Boone's nickname (5)
Slang for (5)
Source of the battle-ax (6)
The headmaster: Mr. _____ (7)
The soldier thinks Omri is a _____. (5)
This wakes Omri up at dawn. (5)
Used as a wash basin for Boone & Little Bear: _____ cup (3)
Used to open Omri's great-grandmother's jewel box (3)
What Adiel accuses Omri of stealing. (6)
What Patrick tells Mr. Johnson (5)
Where Little Bear sleeps his first night alive (5)

Indian In The Cupboard Word Search 3

```
A R R O W S K S P L A S T I C B O O N E
C D R R E X N I E K S D R S W E I H S P
U L I I N O O N N C S T P C O A C R Z M
P Z R E I S T U I A K I N H K C E K M X
B C G T L I C Q C G L T G D O I P Y L
O G A Y K S O O I H P S J T Z J P F R Z
A N J A F T W R L T S E J T I J E K L Q
R S N P M E B I V X B C O E L S T L Z
D O P P H R M I H D O L K H A E L J Q
N L D I C S Y N W Y A S O V N L O N M
N D D T C F Q N J Z R T B O P S I N N J
N I B O W T G J B A N D A G E D L O A G
R E Y P R I U R G E R G R S E I D A N C
S R H S R X F R F A E J S E R Q I F N T
M D S A N L F E E B K F S P A D T K G T
P A T R I C K B R S O B A X N M B E L T
Y R R O Z D S X T X C N J I L M B I I K
A V O N M G Q O P B P J M G Y W A Y A W
X W H C W M H G C Y C U L L A H T G R K
B Q S J W S Y L O N G H O U S E H V T V
```

ADIEL	BOONE	HAIL	PENICILLIN	SPIT
APRIL	BOW	HALLUCY	PICTURES	STARS
ARROW	CHAIN	INDIAN	PLASTIC	STEALING
ART	CHIEF	IROQUOIS	RAT	TEPEE
BANDAGE	COKE	JOHNSON	SCALPS	TOMMY
BEAR	COWBOY	KEY	SEED	TRAIL
BEARD	CRIES	KNIGHT	SHORTS	TRUTH
BEEF	CUPBOARD	KNOT	SHOTS	WIFE
BELT	DREAM	LONGHOUSE	SISTERS	YAPP
BLOOD	EGG	NATIONS	SKATEBOARD	
BOOHOO	GILLON	PATRICK	SOLDIER	

Indian In The Cupboard Word Search 3 Answer Key

ADIEL	BOONE	HAIL	PENICILLIN	SPIT
APRIL	BOW	HALLUCY	PICTURES	STARS
ARROW	CHAIN	INDIAN	PLASTIC	STEALING
ART	CHIEF	IROQUOIS	RAT	TEPEE
BANDAGE	COKE	JOHNSON	SCALPS	TOMMY
BEAR	COWBOY	KEY	SEED	TRAIL
BEARD	CRIES	KNIGHT	SHORTS	TRUTH
BEEF	CUPBOARD	KNOT	SHOTS	WIFE
BELT	DREAM	LONGHOUSE	SISTERS	YAPP
BLOOD	EGG	NATIONS	SKATEBOARD	
BOOHOO	GILLON	PATRICK	SOLDIER	

Indian In The Cupboard Word Search 4

```
B L O O D I N D I A N L V W S G S H B G
C O C U P B O A R D I I O G I T G T E F
Y K O Y N R N R L I A X N R F A R L Q
J K J H H G A P H L R Q O G T E U T G
Y A P P O W T S E I T H S T E R P S
B M P X F O I A C H J P C Q O P V C
W M G L K R O M H D I N I G A J K U E Z
I M K X A H N T A N T B B L W N S E
J R P V S S T L R E K E R P S I T E
P O O A G Z T P L E P A E T S J G S E M
N P H Q T B N I U S R I F M C D H T A Q
J W B N U R B P C S D V C V W S T E L Z
B H J K S O I D Y L Q G B T C E F R I Y
K H H W E O I C O E S G B B U I T S N E
P T O M M Y N S K A T E B O A R D V G D
X V Y A O Z F O R R A N E W A C E A I V
C B E B P E C J P R Q O K D R K D S L X
X R W N I A H C D O L O D T G N M T L
D O R H D M Q H G W Q B A J A O F Q O N
C N C A D I E L I A H R S B N T S M N T
```

ADIEL	BOONE	HAIL	PATRICK	SOLDIER
APRIL	BOW	HALLUCY	PENICILLIN	SPIT
ARROW	CHAIN	HEADDRESS	PICTURES	STARS
ART	CHIEF	INDIAN	PLASTIC	STEALING
BANDAGE	COKE	IROQUOIS	RAT	TEPEE
BEAR	COWBOY	JOHNSON	SCALPS	TOMMY
BEARD	CRIES	KEY	SEED	TRAIL
BEEF	CUPBOARD	KNIGHT	SHORTS	TRUTH
BELT	DREAM	KNOT	SHOTS	WIFE
BLOOD	EGG	LONGHOUSE	SISTERS	YAPP
BOOHOO	GILLON	NATIONS	SKATEBOARD	

Indian In The Cupboard Word Search 4 Answer Key

ADIEL	BOONE	HAIL	PATRICK	SOLDIER
APRIL	BOW	HALLUCY	PENICILLIN	SPIT
ARROW	CHAIN	HEADDRESS	PICTURES	STARS
ART	CHIEF	INDIAN	PLASTIC	STEALING
BANDAGE	COKE	IROQUOIS	RAT	TEPEE
BEAR	COWBOY	JOHNSON	SCALPS	TOMMY
BEARD	CRIES	KEY	SEED	TRAIL
BEEF	CUPBOARD	KNIGHT	SHORTS	TRUTH
BELT	DREAM	KNOT	SHOTS	WIFE
BLOOD	EGG	LONGHOUSE	SISTERS	YAPP
BOOHOO	GILLON	NATIONS	SKATEBOARD	

Indian In The Cupboard Crossword 1

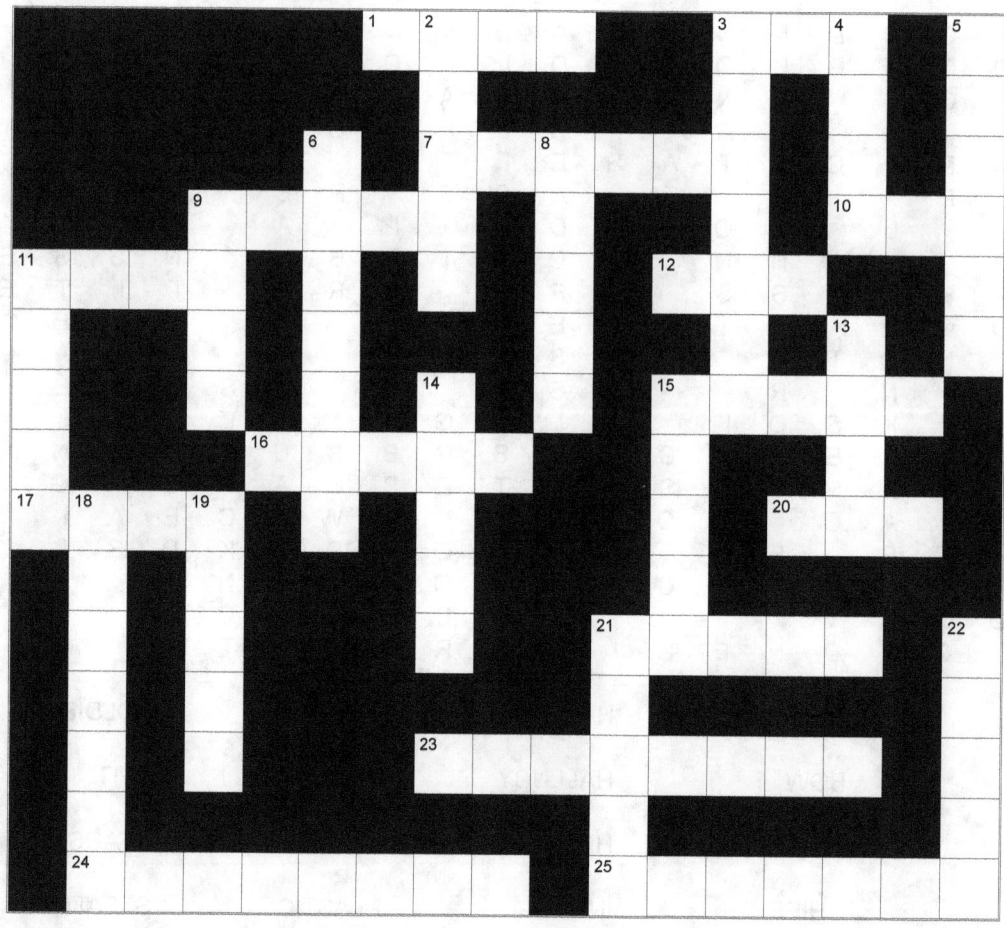

Across

1. Owner of the store where Omri purchased plastic figures
3. Belonged to the dead Indian chief
7. Patrick's birthday gift to Omri: Plastic _____
9. Plastic cowboy who comes to life
10. Used as a wash basin for Boone & Little Bear: _____ cup
11. Drink Omri gave the Indian
12. It was nesting in the floor under Omri's bed.
15. Where Little Bear sleeps his first night alive
16. Slang for
17. Little Bear cooks on this made from an erector set.
20. Boone's best subject in school
21. He died inside the cupboard: Indian _____.
23. Mr. Yapp accused Omri of this.
24. Place where toys come to life
25. Iroquois Indians were sometimes called this: The Five _____.

Down

2. Omri's brother with the missing football shorts
3. What Omri needs from the medical orderly
4. If Omri got him this, Little Bear would dance.
5. Source of the battle-ax
6. He believed Omri was a character in a dream.
8. The soldier thinks Omri is a _____.
9. Omri gave Little Bear canned _____ for breakfast.
11. Reason for Boone's nickname
13. Indian in the cupboard: Little ____
14. Little Bear removes this from Boone's chest.
15. What Patrick tells Mr. Johnson
18. Type of toys that become real in the cupboard.
19. Book Omri reads about Indians: On the _____ of the Iroquois
21. Omri's mother plans to keep the key on this
22. Little Bear's wife: Bright ____

Indian In The Cupboard Crossword 1 Answer Key

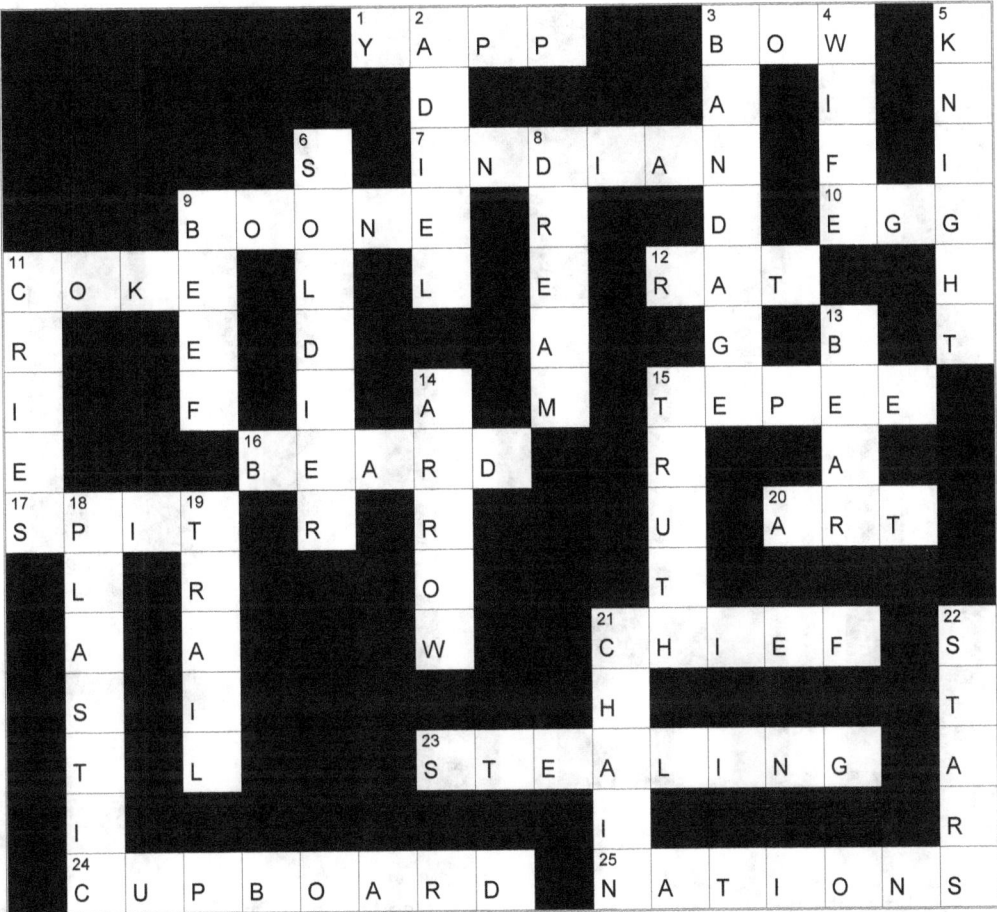

Across
1. Owner of the store where Omri purchased plastic figures
3. Belonged to the dead Indian chief
7. Patrick's birthday gift to Omri: Plastic _____
9. Plastic cowboy who comes to life
10. Used as a wash basin for Boone & Little Bear: _____ cup
11. Drink Omri gave the Indian
12. It was nesting in the floor under Omri's bed.
15. Where Little Bear sleeps his first night alive
16. Slang for
17. Little Bear cooks on this made from an erector set.
20. Boone's best subject in school
21. He died inside the cupboard: Indian _____.
23. Mr. Yapp accused Omri of this.
24. Place where toys come to life
25. Iroquois Indians were sometimes called this: The Five _____.

Down
2. Omri's brother with the missing football shorts
3. What Omri needs from the medical orderly
4. If Omri got him this, Little Bear would dance.
5. Source of the battle-ax
6. He believed Omri was a character in a dream.
8. The soldier thinks Omri is a _____.
9. Omri gave Little Bear canned _____ for breakfast.
11. Reason for Boone's nickname
13. Indian in the cupboard: Little _____
14. Little Bear removes this from Boone's chest.
15. What Patrick tells Mr. Johnson
18. Type of toys that become real in the cupboard.
19. Book Omri reads about Indians: On the _____ of the Iroquois
21. Omri's mother plans to keep the key on this
22. Little Bear's wife: Bright _____

Indian In The Cupboard Crossword 2

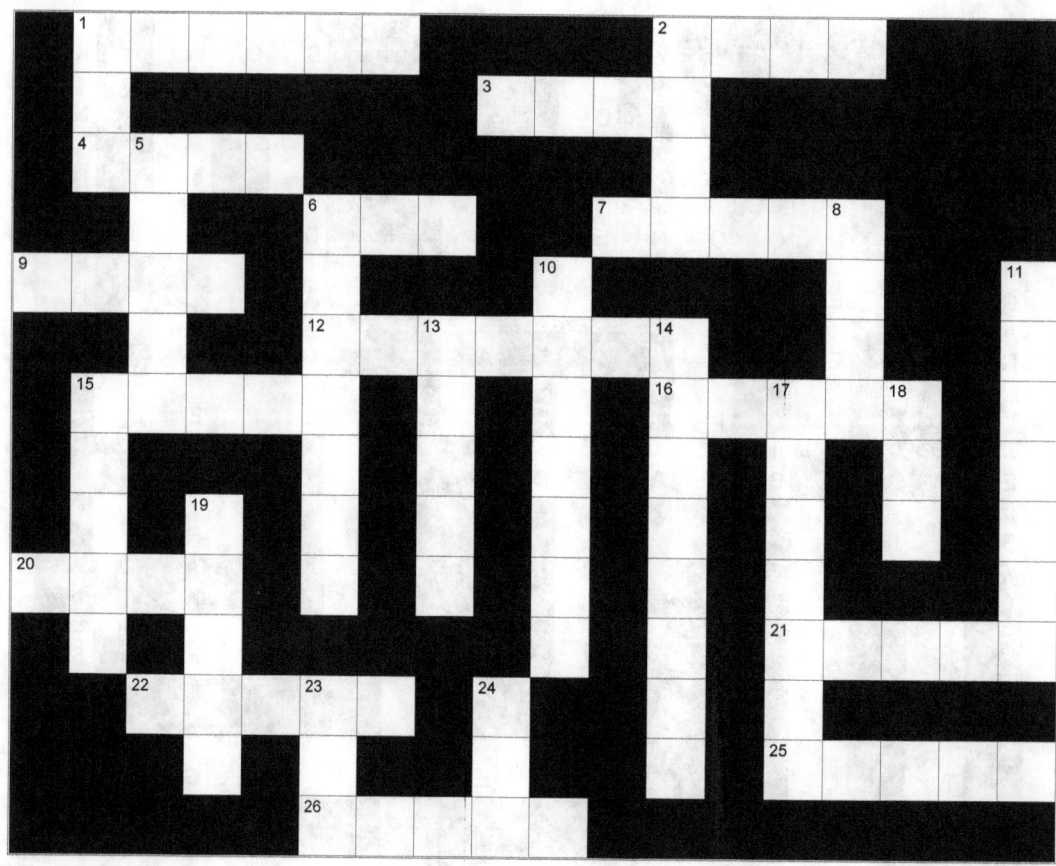

Across
1. Source of the battle-ax
2. Omri gave Little Bear canned _____ for breakfast.
3. Drink Omri gave the Indian
4. Owner of the store where Omri purchased plastic figures
6. Belonged to the dead Indian chief
7. Little Bear removes this from Boone's chest.
9. Little Bear cooks on this made from an erector set.
12. Iroquois Indians were sometimes called this: The Five _____.
15. Little Bear and Omri; Little Bear and Boone are _____ Brothers
16. Where Little Bear sleeps his first night alive
20. Cowboy escapes from the dress-up crate through this
21. First World War soldier
22. The soldier thinks Omri is a _____.
25. He died inside the cupboard: Indian _____.
26. What Patrick tells Mr. Johnson

Down
1. Used to open Omri's great-grandmother's jewel box
2. Indian in the cupboard: Little _____
5. Omri's brother with the missing football shorts
6. What Omri needs from the medical orderly
8. If Omri got him this, Little Bear would dance.
10. He believed Omri was a character in a dream.
11. Boone's nickname for Omri: _____-Nation
13. Book Omri reads about Indians: On the _____ of the Iroquois
14. Mr. Yapp accused Omri of this.
15. Plastic cowboy who comes to life
17. Type of toys that become real in the cupboard.
18. Used as a wash basin for Boone & Little Bear: _____ cup
19. Little Bear's wife: Bright _____
23. Boone's best subject in school
24. It was nesting in the floor under Omri's bed.

Indian In The Cupboard Crossword 2 Answer Key

	1 K	N	I	G	H	T				2 B	E	E	F	
	E							3 C	O	K	E			
	4 Y	5 A	P	P						A				
		D			6 B	O	W		7 A	R	R	O	8 W	
9 S	P	I	T		A			10 S					I	11 H
		E		12 N	13 A	T	I	O	N	14 S			F	A
	15 B	L	O	O	D			R		L		16 T	17 P	18 E	E	L
	O				A			A		D		E	L		G	L
	O		19 S		G			I		E		A		G	U
20 K	N	O	T		E			L		A		L		S	C
	E		A					R				I		21 T	O	M	M	Y
		22 D	R	23 E	A	M		24 R				N		I		
			S		R			A				25 G		C	H	I	E	F
				26 T	R	U	T	H										

Across
1. Source of the battle-ax
2. Omri gave Little Bear canned _____ for breakfast.
3. Drink Omri gave the Indian
4. Owner of the store where Omri purchased plastic figures
6. Belonged to the dead Indian chief
7. Little Bear removes this from Boone's chest.
9. Little Bear cooks on this made from an erector set.
12. Iroquois Indians were sometimes called this: The Five _____.
15. Little Bear and Omri; Little Bear and Boone are _____ Brothers
16. Where Little Bear sleeps his first night alive
20. Cowboy escapes from the dress-up crate through this
21. First World War soldier
22. The soldier thinks Omri is a _____.
25. He died inside the cupboard: Indian _____.
26. What Patrick tells Mr. Johnson

Down
1. Used to open Omri's great-grandmother's jewel box
2. Indian in the cupboard: Little _____
5. Omri's brother with the missing football shorts
6. What Omri needs from the medical orderly
8. If Omri got him this, Little Bear would dance.
10. He believed Omri was a character in a dream.
11. Boone's nickname for Omri: _____-Nation
13. Book Omri reads about Indians: On the _____ of the Iroquois
14. Mr. Yapp accused Omri of this.
15. Plastic cowboy who comes to life
17. Type of toys that become real in the cupboard.
18. Used as a wash basin for Boone & Little Bear: _____ cup
19. Little Bear's wife: Bright _____
23. Boone's best subject in school
24. It was nesting in the floor under Omri's bed.

Indian In The Cupboard Crossword 3

Across
1. Patrick's birthday gift to Omri: Plastic _____
3. This wakes Omri up at dawn.
6. Little Bear gave Omri this as payment for his wife.
8. Girl who teases Patrick at school
9. Place where toys come to life
11. He died inside the cupboard: Indian _____.
12. Omri's brother who gave Omri the cupboard
13. Belonged to the dead Indian chief
14. Owner of the store where Omri purchased plastic figures
16. Little Bear's wife: Bright ____
19. What Omri needs from the medical orderly
21. Little Bear builds his longhouse in the _____ tray.
22. Boone's best subject in school
23. Omri was afraid Little Bear would kill him.
24. Drink Omri gave the Indian
25. Omri's friend

Down
2. The soldier thinks Omri is a _____.
3. Little Bear cooks on this made from an erector set.
4. What Patrick tells Mr. Johnson
5. Little Bear belonged to this tribe.
6. Little Bear and Omri; Little Bear and Boone are _____ Brothers
7. Iroquois house
8. Omri's brother with the missing football shorts
10. Omri gave Little Bear canned _____ for breakfast.
11. Omri's mother plans to keep the key on this
15. Type of toys that become real in the cupboard.
17. First World War soldier
18. It was nesting in the floor under Omri's bed.
19. Indian in the cupboard: Little ____
20. Used as a wash basin for Boone & Little Bear: _____ cup
21. What Adiel accuses Omri of stealing.

Indian In The Cupboard Crossword 3 Answer Key

Across
1. Patrick's birthday gift to Omri: Plastic _____
3. This wakes Omri up at dawn.
6. Little Bear gave Omri this as payment for his wife.
8. Girl who teases Patrick at school
9. Place where toys come to life
11. He died inside the cupboard: Indian _____.
12. Omri's brother who gave Omri the cupboard
13. Belonged to the dead Indian chief
14. Owner of the store where Omri purchased plastic figures
16. Little Bear's wife: Bright ____
19. What Omri needs from the medical orderly
21. Little Bear builds his longhouse in the _____ tray.
22. Boone's best subject in school
23. Omri was afraid Little Bear would kill him.
24. Drink Omri gave the Indian
25. Omri's friend

Down
2. The soldier thinks Omri is a _____.
3. Little Bear cooks on this made from an erector set.
4. What Patrick tells Mr. Johnson
5. Little Bear belonged to this tribe.
6. Little Bear and Omri; Little Bear and Boone are _____ Brothers
7. Iroquois house
8. Omri's brother with the missing football shorts
10. Omri gave Little Bear canned _____ for breakfast.
11. Omri's mother plans to keep the key on this
15. Type of toys that become real in the cupboard.
17. First World War soldier
18. It was nesting in the floor under Omri's bed.
19. Indian in the cupboard: Little ____
20. Used as a wash basin for Boone & Little Bear: _____ cup
21. What Adiel accuses Omri of stealing.

Indian In The Cupboard Crossword 4

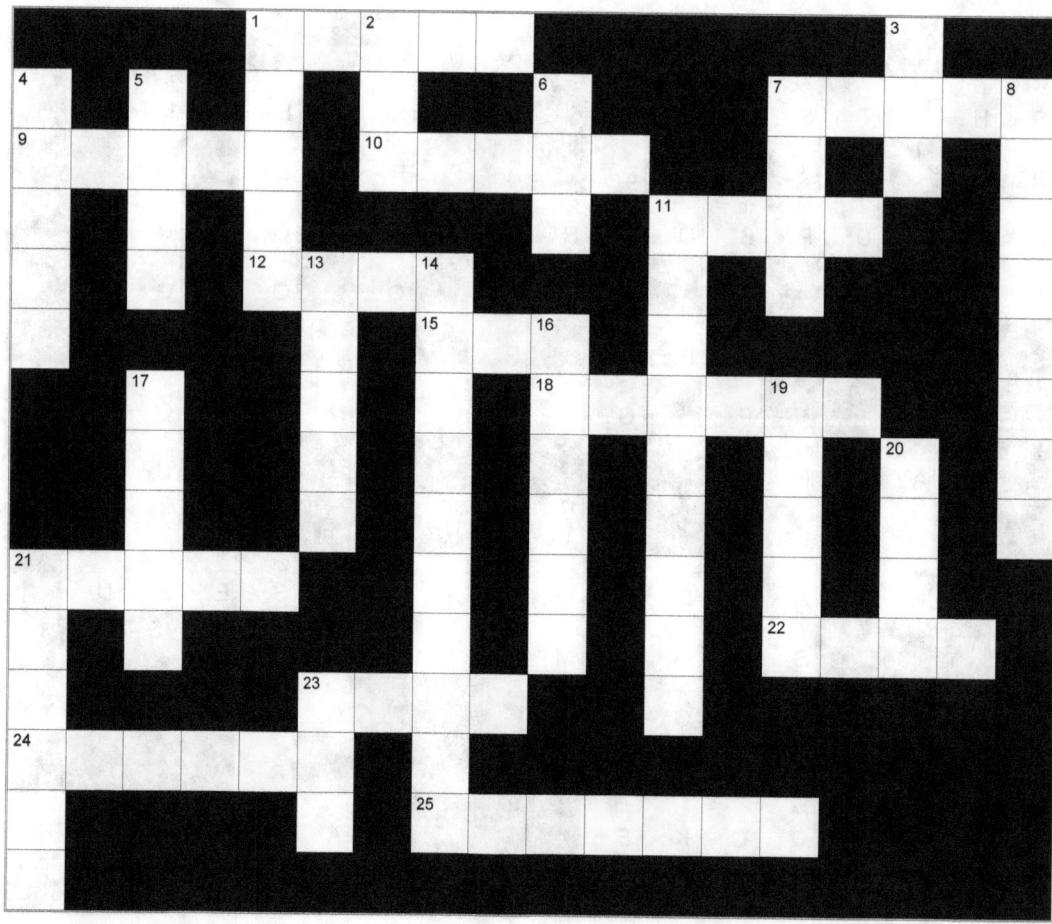

Across

1. Book Omri reads about Indians: On the _____ of the Iroquois
7. Little Bear's wife: Bright ____
9. The soldier thinks Omri is a _____.
10. Where Little Bear sleeps his first night alive
11. It was the size of a football to Little Bear and Boone.
12. Owner of the store where Omri purchased plastic figures
15. Used as a wash basin for Boone & Little Bear: _____ cup
18. Patrick's birthday gift to Omri: Plastic _____
21. Reason for Boone's nickname
22. If Omri got him this, Little Bear would dance.
23. Little Bear gave Omri this as payment for his wife.
24. Boone's nickname
25. Iroquois Indians were sometimes called this: The Five _____.

Down

1. First World War soldier
2. Boone's best subject in school
3. It was nesting in the floor under Omri's bed.
4. Omri's brother with the missing football shorts
5. Indian in the cupboard: Little ____
6. Used to open Omri's great-grandmother's jewel box
7. Little Bear cooks on this made from an erector set.
8. Mr. Yapp accused Omri of this.
11. Little Bear destroys this
13. Girl who teases Patrick at school
14. Not yet discovered in Tommy's time.
16. Omri's brother who gave Omri the cupboard
17. Omri's mother plans to keep the key on this
19. Little Bear removes this from Boone's chest.
20. Omri gave Little Bear canned _____ for breakfast.
21. Omri was afraid Little Bear would kill him.
23. Belonged to the dead Indian chief

Indian In The Cupboard Crossword 4 Answer Key

			1 T	2 R	A	I	L				3 R	
4 A		5 B		O		6 K		7 S	T	A	R	8 S
9 D	R	E	A	M	10 T	E	P	E	E		P		T
I		A		M		Y			11 H	A	I	L	E
E		12 Y	13 A	P	14 P		15 E	16 G	G				A
L		17 C		R	N		I	18 N	D	I	19 A	N	
		H		I	I		L	D			R	20 B	
		A		L	C		L	R			R	E	
21 C	R	I	E	S			O	E			O	E	
O		N					N	S		22 W	I	F	E
W				23 B	E	L	T						
24 B	O	O	H	O									
O				25 W	N	A	T	I	O	N	S		
Y													

Across
1. Book Omri reads about Indians: On the _____ of the Iroquois
7. Little Bear's wife: Bright ____
9. The soldier thinks Omri is a _____.
10. Where Little Bear sleeps his first night alive
11. It was the size of a football to Little Bear and Boone.
12. Owner of the store where Omri purchased plastic figures
15. Used as a wash basin for Boone & Little Bear: _____ cup
18. Patrick's birthday gift to Omri: Plastic _____
21. Reason for Boone's nickname
22. If Omri got him this, Little Bear would dance.
23. Little Bear gave Omri this as payment for his wife.
24. Boone's nickname
25. Iroquois Indians were sometimes called this: The Five _____.

Down
1. First World War soldier
2. Boone's best subject in school
3. It was nesting in the floor under Omri's bed.
4. Omri's brother with the missing football shorts
5. Indian in the cupboard: Little ____
6. Used to open Omri's great-grandmother's jewel box
7. Little Bear cooks on this made from an erector set.
8. Mr. Yapp accused Omri of this.
11. Little Bear destroys this
13. Girl who teases Patrick at school
14. Not yet discovered in Tommy's time.
16. Omri's brother who gave Omri the cupboard
17. Omri's mother plans to keep the key on this
19. Little Bear removes this from Boone's chest.
20. Omri gave Little Bear canned _____ for breakfast.
21. Omri was afraid Little Bear would kill him.
23. Belonged to the dead Indian chief

Indian In The Cupboard

YAPP	ADIEL	SKATEBOARD	STARS	SHORTS
BOW	BOONE	TEPEE	TRAIL	WIFE
COKE	SHOTS	FREE SPACE	PATRICK	KNOT
PICTURES	CUPBOARD	DREAM	SCALPS	SPIT
APRIL	SISTERS	IROQUOIS	TOMMY	BLOOD

Indian In The Cupboard

BELT	BEAR	BANDAGE	HAIL	PENICILLIN
JOHNSON	TRUTH	CHAIN	GILLON	CHIEF
SOLDIER	EGG	FREE SPACE	ARROW	KNIGHT
COWBOY	LONGHOUSE	NATIONS	PLASTIC	INDIAN
RAT	BEEF	HALLUCY	BEARD	SEED

Indian In The Cupboard

SPIT	PICTURES	BLOOD	INDIAN	SOLDIER
NATIONS	KNIGHT	PATRICK	CRIES	STARS
LONGHOUSE	BEAR	FREE SPACE	SKATEBOARD	EGG
SCALPS	BOW	SHORTS	BELT	BOOHOO
KNOT	CHIEF	TEPEE	STEALING	BEEF

Indian In The Cupboard

APRIL	BOONE	ART	COWBOY	SHOTS
JOHNSON	HEADDRESS	TRAIL	ADIEL	CUPBOARD
SEED	PLASTIC	FREE SPACE	SISTERS	BEARD
HALLUCY	CHAIN	RAT	HAIL	YAPP
WIFE	PENICILLIN	KEY	IROQUOIS	DREAM

Indian In The Cupboard

BLOOD	STEALING	WIFE	EGG	INDIAN
TEPEE	JOHNSON	YAPP	SISTERS	SHORTS
BEARD	BOOHOO	FREE SPACE	SOLDIER	CHAIN
KNIGHT	GILLON	CRIES	RAT	STARS
BELT	CHIEF	DREAM	BOW	APRIL

Indian In The Cupboard

TOMMY	SPIT	ARROW	HEADDRESS	SCALPS
KEY	BEEF	BEAR	ADIEL	LONGHOUSE
SKATEBOARD	IROQUOIS	FREE SPACE	SEED	TRUTH
PICTURES	PENICILLIN	CUPBOARD	BANDAGE	KNOT
BOONE	COKE	COWBOY	SHOTS	NATIONS

Indian In The Cupboard

KNIGHT	KNOT	ADIEL	YAPP	JOHNSON
PICTURES	SKATEBOARD	CHAIN	CUPBOARD	TRAIL
TRUTH	SOLDIER	FREE SPACE	KEY	BANDAGE
BELT	BEEF	BEARD	NATIONS	SHOTS
HALLUCY	STEALING	COWBOY	SPIT	BLOOD

Indian In The Cupboard

IROQUOIS	SHORTS	TOMMY	BEAR	HAIL
PATRICK	PENICILLIN	GILLON	EGG	BOONE
BOW	SEED	FREE SPACE	INDIAN	DREAM
ART	STARS	BOOHOO	SISTERS	TEPEE
WIFE	RAT	HEADDRESS	ARROW	CHIEF

Indian In The Cupboard

APRIL	CUPBOARD	IROQUOIS	SEED	YAPP
ART	BOONE	SHOTS	BOW	COKE
GILLON	DREAM	FREE SPACE	EGG	SKATEBOARD
TRUTH	ARROW	BEAR	COWBOY	BOOHOO
KNOT	TEPEE	PICTURES	SHORTS	SPIT

Indian In The Cupboard

SISTERS	BEEF	PATRICK	KNIGHT	PLASTIC
WIFE	HALLUCY	BANDAGE	TRAIL	NATIONS
INDIAN	RAT	FREE SPACE	PENICILLIN	KEY
SOLDIER	CHAIN	STARS	LONGHOUSE	HEADDRESS
HAIL	TOMMY	STEALING	CHIEF	JOHNSON

Indian In The Cupboard

LONGHOUSE	KEY	SCALPS	BLOOD	NATIONS
BANDAGE	WIFE	TRAIL	SHOTS	HAIL
COKE	YAPP	FREE SPACE	TRUTH	DREAM
PICTURES	BEEF	IROQUOIS	SISTERS	RAT
BOONE	ADIEL	STARS	PLASTIC	BOOHOO

Indian In The Cupboard

HEADDRESS	PENICILLIN	KNIGHT	PATRICK	APRIL
ARROW	CHAIN	STEALING	BOW	SEED
SKATEBOARD	SHORTS	FREE SPACE	SOLDIER	BEARD
TOMMY	INDIAN	JOHNSON	SPIT	CUPBOARD
CHIEF	ART	KNOT	BELT	EGG

Indian In The Cupboard

LONGHOUSE	KEY	TEPEE	BOONE	SCALPS
HALLUCY	BOOHOO	JOHNSON	SHORTS	BEAR
PENICILLIN	ART	FREE SPACE	SEED	SHOTS
DREAM	INDIAN	TRAIL	STARS	KNIGHT
BELT	BOW	WIFE	APRIL	NATIONS

Indian In The Cupboard

BLOOD	SKATEBOARD	YAPP	IROQUOIS	KNOT
RAT	COWBOY	SPIT	CHAIN	PICTURES
HEADDRESS	CHIEF	FREE SPACE	STEALING	TOMMY
PLASTIC	BEARD	BANDAGE	SOLDIER	COKE
ADIEL	CUPBOARD	EGG	GILLON	TRUTH

Indian In The Cupboard

ART	PICTURES	TOMMY	CHAIN	SHOTS
STEALING	DREAM	SISTERS	EGG	HAIL
PENICILLIN	APRIL	FREE SPACE	TRUTH	SOLDIER
HEADDRESS	IROQUOIS	SPIT	PLASTIC	YAPP
CRIES	BOOHOO	KEY	BOW	CHIEF

Indian In The Cupboard

GILLON	ADIEL	HALLUCY	RAT	BLOOD
ARROW	BEARD	TEPEE	LONGHOUSE	STARS
NATIONS	PATRICK	FREE SPACE	JOHNSON	INDIAN
BELT	SEED	COWBOY	SKATEBOARD	CUPBOARD
WIFE	COKE	KNIGHT	BEAR	SHORTS

Indian In The Cupboard

HALLUCY	KEY	SISTERS	INDIAN	CHIEF
TEPEE	TRAIL	SKATEBOARD	SCALPS	NATIONS
BOW	BEAR	FREE SPACE	STEALING	YAPP
TRUTH	SHORTS	CUPBOARD	BEEF	PLASTIC
STARS	BOONE	DREAM	LONGHOUSE	GILLON

Indian In The Cupboard

COWBOY	KNOT	ART	TOMMY	APRIL
EGG	ARROW	IROQUOIS	BANDAGE	BOOHOO
HEADDRESS	SEED	FREE SPACE	SHOTS	KNIGHT
BELT	COKE	CRIES	HAIL	JOHNSON
PATRICK	SOLDIER	BLOOD	CHAIN	PICTURES

Indian In The Cupboard

KNIGHT	SCALPS	SEED	HALLUCY	SPIT
DREAM	TRAIL	ARROW	BANDAGE	PATRICK
BEAR	JOHNSON	FREE SPACE	COWBOY	TOMMY
IROQUOIS	BEARD	BLOOD	SKATEBOARD	INDIAN
PENICILLIN	TRUTH	HEADDRESS	RAT	KNOT

Indian In The Cupboard

KEY	ADIEL	STEALING	PLASTIC	BOW
HAIL	CRIES	BOONE	TEPEE	NATIONS
BOOHOO	SOLDIER	FREE SPACE	PICTURES	BEEF
EGG	ART	SISTERS	CHIEF	BELT
STARS	GILLON	CUPBOARD	SHOTS	LONGHOUSE

Indian In The Cupboard

KEY	TOMMY	COKE	BANDAGE	ART
EGG	BELT	STARS	APRIL	BEARD
HAIL	KNOT	FREE SPACE	SPIT	SISTERS
COWBOY	SHORTS	ARROW	SOLDIER	SCALPS
BOW	BEAR	BOOHOO	CRIES	BOONE

Indian In The Cupboard

WIFE	HALLUCY	DREAM	SKATEBOARD	TRUTH
TRAIL	PICTURES	SHOTS	RAT	CHIEF
TEPEE	INDIAN	FREE SPACE	CUPBOARD	PENICILLIN
HEADDRESS	KNIGHT	LONGHOUSE	SEED	BLOOD
ADIEL	NATIONS	IROQUOIS	GILLON	BEEF

Indian In The Cupboard

SOLDIER	BOOHOO	EGG	SCALPS	APRIL
SHOTS	BLOOD	CHIEF	NATIONS	PATRICK
LONGHOUSE	KNOT	FREE SPACE	BOW	BEAR
STARS	KEY	HEADDRESS	TRUTH	SHORTS
DREAM	BANDAGE	ART	RAT	BELT

Indian In The Cupboard

SISTERS	TOMMY	BOONE	KNIGHT	JOHNSON
PLASTIC	WIFE	HALLUCY	INDIAN	YAPP
COKE	COWBOY	FREE SPACE	BEEF	TEPEE
CHAIN	PENICILLIN	TRAIL	ADIEL	BEARD
IROQUOIS	CRIES	ARROW	PICTURES	SEED

Indian In The Cupboard

PLASTIC	IROQUOIS	BLOOD	KNIGHT	SPIT
HAIL	BOOHOO	SHORTS	SKATEBOARD	TOMMY
CHAIN	BANDAGE	FREE SPACE	CUPBOARD	WIFE
SHOTS	GILLON	LONGHOUSE	STARS	NATIONS
ADIEL	ART	EGG	BELT	COKE

Indian In The Cupboard

PENICILLIN	SOLDIER	CRIES	JOHNSON	CHIEF
SCALPS	KEY	PATRICK	INDIAN	BOONE
SISTERS	TRAIL	FREE SPACE	BOW	DREAM
COWBOY	BEAR	BEEF	YAPP	RAT
ARROW	KNOT	HALLUCY	TEPEE	TRUTH

Indian In The Cupboard

BELT	IROQUOIS	ART	KNIGHT	PENICILLIN
DREAM	CHAIN	TEPEE	BOW	JOHNSON
PATRICK	SKATEBOARD	FREE SPACE	SEED	SPIT
SCALPS	HAIL	BLOOD	CHIEF	ADIEL
STEALING	HEADDRESS	ARROW	PLASTIC	CUPBOARD

Indian In The Cupboard

WIFE	CRIES	NATIONS	TOMMY	PICTURES
SISTERS	TRAIL	BOOHOO	SHOTS	COKE
YAPP	COWBOY	FREE SPACE	LONGHOUSE	KNOT
APRIL	BEAR	STARS	SHORTS	RAT
HALLUCY	BEARD	GILLON	BANDAGE	BEEF

Indian In The Cupboard

BEEF	BELT	SPIT	IROQUOIS	KNOT
JOHNSON	SEED	COKE	BOW	BLOOD
DREAM	ART	FREE SPACE	HEADDRESS	CUPBOARD
SCALPS	STEALING	BOOHOO	KEY	PICTURES
TOMMY	RAT	BOONE	TRAIL	INDIAN

Indian In The Cupboard

TEPEE	HAIL	SHOTS	BANDAGE	STARS
TRUTH	LONGHOUSE	SKATEBOARD	YAPP	KNIGHT
HALLUCY	NATIONS	FREE SPACE	COWBOY	PENICILLIN
ARROW	BEARD	APRIL	GILLON	PLASTIC
CHIEF	ADIEL	BEAR	CHAIN	CRIES

Indian In The Cupboard

COKE	SHOTS	YAPP	BOOHOO	HAIL
BEAR	CRIES	APRIL	IROQUOIS	BELT
JOHNSON	GILLON	FREE SPACE	SCALPS	TOMMY
EGG	PATRICK	SPIT	CUPBOARD	ADIEL
LONGHOUSE	PLASTIC	TRAIL	CHIEF	TEPEE

Indian In The Cupboard

BEEF	SISTERS	BANDAGE	CHAIN	KNOT
SEED	HEADDRESS	RAT	TRUTH	STEALING
SOLDIER	PICTURES	FREE SPACE	WIFE	COWBOY
ART	SHORTS	SKATEBOARD	INDIAN	BEARD
STARS	NATIONS	HALLUCY	KEY	BOONE

Indian In The Cupboard Vocabulary Word List

No.	Word	Clue/Definition
1.	AGHAST	Overcome with shock
2.	APPALLED	Shocked
3.	APPREHENSION	A feeling of anxiety or fear that something bad is going to occur
4.	BAFFLEMENT	Bewilderment
5.	BANDOLIER	A kind of belt worn over one shoulder and across the chest
6.	BEMUSED	Puzzled
7.	BRIDLE	A set of leather straps fitted to a horse's head that includes the bit and the reins
8.	COAXED	Persuaded gently
9.	COHERENT	Logical
10.	DEFIANT	Tending to confront and challenge
11.	DESPAIR	A feeling of hopelessness
12.	DISMAY	To dishearten, alarm, cause loss of courage
13.	FIENDISH	Devilish
14.	FLUMMOXED	Perplexed
15.	FOREBODING	A feeling that something bad is going to happen
16.	GALVANIZED	Stimulated into great activity
17.	GAPED	Stared in open-mouthed surprise
18.	HECTORING	Speaking in a domineering tone
19.	IMPERIOUSLY	Domineeringly
20.	INCREDULOUS	Unbelieving
21.	INFURIATED	Enraged
22.	INTRICATE	Containing many details or small parts that are skillfully made
23.	JOISTS	Floor, roof, or ceiling supports
24.	LITHELY	Bending easily
25.	LONGHOUSE	A long, bark-covered dwelling place built by some Native North American peoples, esp. the Iroquois
26.	MAGNANIMOUSLY	Nobly
27.	MAIZE	Corn
28.	MINUTE	Extremely small
29.	MULISH	Unwilling to cooperate or listen to suggestions
30.	MYRIAD	Numerous
31.	OBLIGED	Indebted to do something for someone
32.	OMNIVOROUS	Eating any kind of food, including both plants and animals
33.	PEEVISHLY	Irritably
34.	PENCE	Plural of penny
35.	PERILS	Sources of potential harm
36.	PERSECUTOR	Oppressor; tyrant
37.	PETRIFIED	Immobile with fear
38.	RACUOUS	Loud and hoarse or unpleasant-sounding
39.	RANSACKED	Searched thoroughly but handled carelessly
40.	RAPTURE	A euphoric state in which somebody is overwhelmed by happiness and unaware of anything else
41.	RAVENOUSLY	Hungrily
42.	REGRETFULLY	Remorsefully
43.	RELAPSE	To fall ill again after seeming to have made a recovery
44.	RELUCTANT	Hesitant
45.	RESTIVE	Having little patience and on the verge of resisting control
46.	RETORTED	Replied in quick response to something someone has said
47.	SAGEBRUSH	Plant native to North America with silvery wedge-shaped

		leaves and clusters of small white flowers
48.	SCALPS	The skin and hair covering the skulls of enemies; cut off as trophies
49.	SCORN	A feeling of dislike
50.	SEPTIC	Full of pus
51.	SNIDE	Sarcastic
52.	SPIT	A thin rod or bar on which meat is pierced for broiling or roasting over a fire
53.	TACTICS	A course of action to achieve short-term gains
54.	TETHERED	Tied with a rope or chain
55.	TOURNIQUET	A tight band applied around an arm or a leg to stop bleeding
56.	TRANSFIXED	Made motionless
57.	TRANSFUSION	The transfer of blood into the bloodstream of somebody who has lost blood
58.	TRUCE	An agreed break in any type of dispute or feud
59.	UNCOMPROMISINGLY	Unwilling to back down
60.	UNWARILY	Not cautiously
61.	VULNERABLE	Open to physical danger or harm

Indian in the Cupboard Vocabulary Fill In The Blanks 1

_____ 1. Remorsefully

_____ 2. Bending easily

_____ 3. Sources of potential harm

_____ 4. Searched thoroughly but handled carelessly

_____ 5. Unwilling to cooperate or listen to suggestions

_____ 6. To fall ill again after seeming to have made a recovery

_____ 7. An agreed break in any type of dispute or feud

_____ 8. A set of leather straps fitted to a horse's head that includes the bit and the reins

_____ 9. Eating any kind of food, including both plants and animals

_____ 10. Extremely small

_____ 11. Perplexed

_____ 12. Oppressor; tyrant

_____ 13. Stimulated into great activity

_____ 14. The transfer of blood into the bloodstream of somebody who has lost blood

_____ 15. Devilish

_____ 16. Speaking in a domineering tone

_____ 17. Replied in quick response to something someone has said

_____ 18. Unwilling to back down

_____ 19. A kind of belt worn over one shoulder and across the chest

_____ 20. Enraged

Indian in the Cupboard Vocabulary Fill In The Blanks 1 Answer Key

REGRETFULLY	1. Remorsefully
LITHELY	2. Bending easily
PERILS	3. Sources of potential harm
RANSACKED	4. Searched thoroughly but handled carelessly
MULISH	5. Unwilling to cooperate or listen to suggestions
RELAPSE	6. To fall ill again after seeming to have made a recovery
TRUCE	7. An agreed break in any type of dispute or feud
BRIDLE	8. A set of leather straps fitted to a horse's head that includes the bit and the reins
OMNIVOROUS	9. Eating any kind of food, including both plants and animals
MINUTE	10. Extremely small
FLUMMOXED	11. Perplexed
PERSECUTOR	12. Oppressor; tyrant
GALVANIZED	13. Stimulated into great activity
TRANSFUSION	14. The transfer of blood into the bloodstream of somebody who has lost blood
FIENDISH	15. Devilish
HECTORING	16. Speaking in a domineering tone
RETORTED	17. Replied in quick response to something someone has said
UNCOMPROMISINGLY	18. Unwilling to back down
BANDOLIER	19. A kind of belt worn over one shoulder and across the chest
INFURIATED	20. Enraged

Indian in the Cupboard Vocabulary Fill In The Blanks 2

_____ 1. Hesitant

_____ 2. A long, bark-covered dwelling place built by some Native North American peoples, esp. the Iroquois

_____ 3. Indebted to do something for someone

_____ 4. Shocked

_____ 5. Containing many details or small parts that are skillfully made

_____ 6. Nobly

_____ 7. Open to physical danger or harm

_____ 8. Corn

_____ 9. Searched thoroughly but handled carelessly

_____ 10. Eating any kind of food, including both plants and animals

_____ 11. Tending to confront and challenge

_____ 12. A feeling of anxiety or fear that something bad is going to occur

_____ 13. A euphoric state in which somebody is overwhelmed by happiness and unaware of anything else

_____ 14. Stared in open-mouthed surprise

_____ 15. Persuaded gently

_____ 16. Replied in quick response to something someone has said

_____ 17. Devilish

_____ 18. Unbelieving

_____ 19. Unwilling to back down

_____ 20. A course of action to achieve short-term gains

Indian in the Cupboard Vocabulary Fill In The Blanks 2 Answer Key

RELUCTANT	1. Hesitant
LONGHOUSE	2. A long, bark-covered dwelling place built by some Native North American peoples, esp. the Iroquois
OBLIGED	3. Indebted to do something for someone
APPALLED	4. Shocked
INTRICATE	5. Containing many details or small parts that are skillfully made
MAGNANIMOUSLY	6. Nobly
VULNERABLE	7. Open to physical danger or harm
MAIZE	8. Corn
RANSACKED	9. Searched thoroughly but handled carelessly
OMNIVOROUS	10. Eating any kind of food, including both plants and animals
DEFIANT	11. Tending to confront and challenge
APPREHENSION	12. A feeling of anxiety or fear that something bad is going to occur
RAPTURE	13. A euphoric state in which somebody is overwhelmed by happiness and unaware of anything else
GAPED	14. Stared in open-mouthed surprise
COAXED	15. Persuaded gently
RETORTED	16. Replied in quick response to something someone has said
FIENDISH	17. Devilish
INCREDULOUS	18. Unbelieving
UNCOMPROMISINGLY	19. Unwilling to back down
TACTICS	20. A course of action to achieve short-term gains

Indian in the Cupboard Vocabulary Fill In The Blanks 3

_____ 1. Floor, roof, or ceiling supports

_____ 2. Tied with a rope or chain

_____ 3. Eating any kind of food, including both plants and animals

_____ 4. A euphoric state in which somebody is overwhelmed by happiness and unaware of anything else

_____ 5. Having little patience and on the verge of resisting control

_____ 6. Shocked

_____ 7. Hungrily

_____ 8. Unbelieving

_____ 9. Nobly

_____ 10. Persuaded gently

_____ 11. Perplexed

_____ 12. Overcome with shock

_____ 13. Remorsefully

_____ 14. Bewilderment

_____ 15. Logical

_____ 16. A course of action to achieve short-term gains

_____ 17. A feeling that something bad is going to happen

_____ 18. Irritably

_____ 19. Plant native to North America with silvery wedge-shaped leaves and clusters of small white flowers

_____ 20. A kind of belt worn over one shoulder and across the chest

Indian in the Cupboard Vocabulary Fill In The Blanks 3 Answer Key

JOISTS	1. Floor, roof, or ceiling supports
TETHERED	2. Tied with a rope or chain
OMNIVOROUS	3. Eating any kind of food, including both plants and animals
RAPTURE	4. A euphoric state in which somebody is overwhelmed by happiness and unaware of anything else
RESTIVE	5. Having little patience and on the verge of resisting control
APPALLED	6. Shocked
RAVENOUSLY	7. Hungrily
INCREDULOUS	8. Unbelieving
MAGNANIMOUSLY	9. Nobly
COAXED	10. Persuaded gently
FLUMMOXED	11. Perplexed
AGHAST	12. Overcome with shock
REGRETFULLY	13. Remorsefully
BAFFLEMENT	14. Bewilderment
COHERENT	15. Logical
TACTICS	16. A course of action to achieve short-term gains
FOREBODING	17. A feeling that something bad is going to happen
PEEVISHLY	18. Irritably
SAGEBRUSH	19. Plant native to North America with silvery wedge-shaped leaves and clusters of small white flowers
BANDOLIER	20. A kind of belt worn over one shoulder and across the chest

Indian in the Cupboard Vocabulary Fill In The Blanks 4

_____ 1. Unbelieving

_____ 2. Nobly

_____ 3. Tied with a rope or chain

_____ 4. Stimulated into great activity

_____ 5. Open to physical danger or harm

_____ 6. Containing many details or small parts that are skillfully made

_____ 7. Plant native to North America with silvery wedge-shaped leaves and clusters of small white flowers

_____ 8. A kind of belt worn over one shoulder and across the chest

_____ 9. Puzzled

_____ 10. An agreed break in any type of dispute or feud

_____ 11. Hungrily

_____ 12. Persuaded gently

_____ 13. Plural of penny

_____ 14. Made motionless

_____ 15. To dishearten, alarm, cause loss of courage

_____ 16. A thin rod or bar on which meat is pierced for broiling or roasting over a fire

_____ 17. The skin and hair covering the skulls of enemies; cut off as trophies

_____ 18. Loud and hoarse or unpleasant-sounding

_____ 19. A feeling of dislike

_____ 20. Unwilling to back down

Indian in the Cupboard Vocabulary Fill In The Blanks 4 Answer Key

INCREDULOUS	1. Unbelieving
MAGNANIMOUSLY	2. Nobly
TETHERED	3. Tied with a rope or chain
GALVANIZED	4. Stimulated into great activity
VULNERABLE	5. Open to physical danger or harm
INTRICATE	6. Containing many details or small parts that are skillfully made
SAGEBRUSH	7. Plant native to North America with silvery wedge-shaped leaves and clusters of small white flowers
BANDOLIER	8. A kind of belt worn over one shoulder and across the chest
BEMUSED	9. Puzzled
TRUCE	10. An agreed break in any type of dispute or feud
RAVENOUSLY	11. Hungrily
COAXED	12. Persuaded gently
PENCE	13. Plural of penny
TRANSFIXED	14. Made motionless
DISMAY	15. To dishearten, alarm, cause loss of courage
SPIT	16. A thin rod or bar on which meat is pierced for broiling or roasting over a fire
SCALPS	17. The skin and hair covering the skulls of enemies; cut off as trophies
RACUOUS	18. Loud and hoarse or unpleasant-sounding
SCORN	19. A feeling of dislike
UNCOMPROMISINGLY	20. Unwilling to back down

Indian in the Cupboard Vocabulary Matching 1

___ 1. FIENDISH
___ 2. FLUMMOXED
___ 3. COHERENT
___ 4. TOURNIQUET
___ 5. APPREHENSION
___ 6. SPIT
___ 7. RAVENOUSLY
___ 8. SAGEBRUSH
___ 9. DISMAY
___ 10. SCORN
___ 11. RESTIVE
___ 12. BRIDLE
___ 13. VULNERABLE
___ 14. RETORTED
___ 15. PERSECUTOR
___ 16. BEMUSED
___ 17. COAXED
___ 18. LITHELY
___ 19. UNCOMPROMISINGLY
___ 20. TACTICS
___ 21. MAGNANIMOUSLY
___ 22. MAIZE
___ 23. INTRICATE
___ 24. UNWARILY
___ 25. SEPTIC

A. A thin rod or bar on which meat is pierced for broiling or roasting over a fire
B. A tight band applied around an arm or a leg to stop bleeding
C. Corn
D. Unwilling to back down
E. Oppressor; tyrant
F. A course of action to achieve short-term gains
G. Devilish
H. Open to physical danger or harm
I. Replied in quick response to something someone has said
J. A feeling of anxiety or fear that something bad is going to occur
K. Perplexed
L. Logical
M. Plant native to North America with silvery wedge-shaped leaves and clusters of small white flowers
N. Puzzled
O. Having little patience and on the verge of resisting control
P. To dishearten, alarm, cause loss of courage
Q. Nobly
R. Hungrily
S. Bending easily
T. Full of pus
U. Not cautiously
V. A set of leather straps fitted to a horse's head that includes the bit and the reins
W. Persuaded gently
X. Containing many details or small parts that are skillfully made
Y. A feeling of dislike

Indian in the Cupboard Vocabulary Matching 1 Answer Key

G - 1. FIENDISH
K - 2. FLUMMOXED
L - 3. COHERENT
B - 4. TOURNIQUET
J - 5. APPREHENSION
A - 6. SPIT
R - 7. RAVENOUSLY
M - 8. SAGEBRUSH
P - 9. DISMAY
Y - 10. SCORN
O - 11. RESTIVE
V - 12. BRIDLE
H - 13. VULNERABLE
I - 14. RETORTED
E - 15. PERSECUTOR
N - 16. BEMUSED
W - 17. COAXED
S - 18. LITHELY
D - 19. UNCOMPROMISINGLY
F - 20. TACTICS
Q - 21. MAGNANIMOUSLY
C - 22. MAIZE
X - 23. INTRICATE
U - 24. UNWARILY
T - 25. SEPTIC

A. A thin rod or bar on which meat is pierced for broiling or roasting over a fire
B. A tight band applied around an arm or a leg to stop bleeding
C. Corn
D. Unwilling to back down
E. Oppressor; tyrant
F. A course of action to achieve short-term gains
G. Devilish
H. Open to physical danger or harm
I. Replied in quick response to something someone has said
J. A feeling of anxiety or fear that something bad is going to occur
K. Perplexed
L. Logical
M. Plant native to North America with silvery wedge-shaped leaves and clusters of small white flowers
N. Puzzled
O. Having little patience and on the verge of resisting control
P. To dishearten, alarm, cause loss of courage
Q. Nobly
R. Hungrily
S. Bending easily
T. Full of pus
U. Not cautiously
V. A set of leather straps fitted to a horse's head that includes the bit and the reins
W. Persuaded gently
X. Containing many details or small parts that are skillfully made
Y. A feeling of dislike

Indian in the Cupboard Vocabulary Matching 2

___ 1. OMNIVOROUS
___ 2. COHERENT
___ 3. APPREHENSION
___ 4. GAPED
___ 5. REGRETFULLY
___ 6. MULISH
___ 7. JOISTS
___ 8. SPIT
___ 9. DESPAIR
___ 10. TOURNIQUET
___ 11. MAIZE
___ 12. BRIDLE
___ 13. MAGNANIMOUSLY
___ 14. RAPTURE
___ 15. TRANSFIXED
___ 16. FIENDISH
___ 17. HECTORING
___ 18. BEMUSED
___ 19. SNIDE
___ 20. PERSECUTOR
___ 21. BAFFLEMENT
___ 22. TRANSFUSION
___ 23. MYRIAD
___ 24. UNCOMPROMISINGLY
___ 25. RETORTED

A. Made motionless
B. Eating any kind of food, including both plants and animals
C. A tight band applied around an arm or a leg to stop bleeding
D. Sarcastic
E. Replied in quick response to something someone has said
F. Unwilling to cooperate or listen to suggestions
G. The transfer of blood into the bloodstream of somebody who has lost blood
H. Unwilling to back down
I. A set of leather straps fitted to a horse's head that includes the bit and the reins
J. Logical
K. Numerous
L. Puzzled
M. Floor, roof, or ceiling supports
N. Stared in open-mouthed surprise
O. A euphoric state in which somebody is overwhelmed by happiness and unaware of anything else
P. Devilish
Q. A thin rod or bar on which meat is pierced for broiling or roasting over a fire
R. Remorsefully
S. Nobly
T. Oppressor; tyrant
U. Corn
V. Speaking in a domineering tone
W. Bewilderment
X. A feeling of hopelessness
Y. A feeling of anxiety or fear that something bad is going to occur

Indian in the Cupboard Vocabulary Matching 2 Answer Key

B - 1. OMNIVOROUS
J - 2. COHERENT
Y - 3. APPREHENSION
N - 4. GAPED
R - 5. REGRETFULLY
F - 6. MULISH
M - 7. JOISTS
Q - 8. SPIT
X - 9. DESPAIR
C - 10. TOURNIQUET
U - 11. MAIZE
I - 12. BRIDLE
S - 13. MAGNANIMOUSLY
O - 14. RAPTURE
A - 15. TRANSFIXED
P - 16. FIENDISH
V - 17. HECTORING
L - 18. BEMUSED
D - 19. SNIDE
T - 20. PERSECUTOR
W - 21. BAFFLEMENT
G - 22. TRANSFUSION
K - 23. MYRIAD
H - 24. UNCOMPROMISINGLY
E - 25. RETORTED

A. Made motionless
B. Eating any kind of food, including both plants and animals
C. A tight band applied around an arm or a leg to stop bleeding
D. Sarcastic
E. Replied in quick response to something someone has said
F. Unwilling to cooperate or listen to suggestions
G. The transfer of blood into the bloodstream of somebody who has lost blood
H. Unwilling to back down
I. A set of leather straps fitted to a horse's head that includes the bit and the reins
J. Logical
K. Numerous
L. Puzzled
M. Floor, roof, or ceiling supports
N. Stared in open-mouthed surprise
O. A euphoric state in which somebody is overwhelmed by happiness and unaware of anything else
P. Devilish
Q. A thin rod or bar on which meat is pierced for broiling or roasting over a fire
R. Remorsefully
S. Nobly
T. Oppressor; tyrant
U. Corn
V. Speaking in a domineering tone
W. Bewilderment
X. A feeling of hopelessness
Y. A feeling of anxiety or fear that something bad is going to occur

Indian in the Cupboard Vocabulary Matching 3

___ 1. BEMUSED
___ 2. MAIZE
___ 3. RELUCTANT
___ 4. PENCE
___ 5. TRANSFIXED
___ 6. FOREBODING
___ 7. PEEVISHLY
___ 8. TETHERED
___ 9. REGRETFULLY
___ 10. RAPTURE
___ 11. DESPAIR
___ 12. PERSECUTOR
___ 13. VULNERABLE
___ 14. INTRICATE
___ 15. RAVENOUSLY
___ 16. TACTICS
___ 17. RESTIVE
___ 18. RETORTED
___ 19. LITHELY
___ 20. PERILS
___ 21. GAPED
___ 22. BRIDLE
___ 23. TRANSFUSION
___ 24. RANSACKED
___ 25. JOISTS

A. Corn
B. Open to physical danger or harm
C. Made motionless
D. Puzzled
E. Plural of penny
F. Having little patience and on the verge of resisting control
G. A feeling that something bad is going to happen
H. Tied with a rope or chain
I. Containing many details or small parts that are skillfully made
J. Floor, roof, or ceiling supports
K. Searched thoroughly but handled carelessly
L. Sources of potential harm
M. A set of leather straps fitted to a horse's head that includes the bit and the reins
N. A feeling of hopelessness
O. Stared in open-mouthed surprise
P. Hesitant
Q. A course of action to achieve short-term gains
R. Replied in quick response to something someone has said
S. The transfer of blood into the bloodstream of somebody who has lost blood
T. Hungrily
U. Irritably
V. A euphoric state in which somebody is overwhelmed by happiness and unaware of anything else
W. Oppressor; tyrant
X. Remorsefully
Y. Bending easily

Indian in the Cupboard Vocabulary Matching 3 Answer Key

D - 1. BEMUSED
A - 2. MAIZE
P - 3. RELUCTANT
E - 4. PENCE
C - 5. TRANSFIXED
G - 6. FOREBODING
U - 7. PEEVISHLY
H - 8. TETHERED
X - 9. REGRETFULLY
V - 10. RAPTURE
N - 11. DESPAIR
W - 12. PERSECUTOR
B - 13. VULNERABLE
I - 14. INTRICATE
T - 15. RAVENOUSLY
Q - 16. TACTICS
F - 17. RESTIVE
R - 18. RETORTED
Y - 19. LITHELY
L - 20. PERILS
O - 21. GAPED
M - 22. BRIDLE
S - 23. TRANSFUSION
K - 24. RANSACKED
J - 25. JOISTS

A. Corn
B. Open to physical danger or harm
C. Made motionless
D. Puzzled
E. Plural of penny
F. Having little patience and on the verge of resisting control
G. A feeling that something bad is going to happen
H. Tied with a rope or chain
I. Containing many details or small parts that are skillfully made
J. Floor, roof, or ceiling supports
K. Searched thoroughly but handled carelessly
L. Sources of potential harm
M. A set of leather straps fitted to a horse's head that includes the bit and the reins
N. A feeling of hopelessness
O. Stared in open-mouthed surprise
P. Hesitant
Q. A course of action to achieve short-term gains
R. Replied in quick response to something someone has said
S. The transfer of blood into the bloodstream of somebody who has lost blood
T. Hungrily
U. Irritably
V. A euphoric state in which somebody is overwhelmed by happiness and unaware of anything else
W. Oppressor; tyrant
X. Remorsefully
Y. Bending easily

Indian in the Cupboard Vocabulary Matching 4

___ 1. RANSACKED
___ 2. GALVANIZED
___ 3. INCREDULOUS
___ 4. TACTICS
___ 5. LONGHOUSE
___ 6. PERILS
___ 7. SPIT
___ 8. BEMUSED
___ 9. COAXED
___ 10. IMPERIOUSLY
___ 11. SCORN
___ 12. SNIDE
___ 13. MULISH
___ 14. RETORTED
___ 15. DEFIANT
___ 16. UNWARILY
___ 17. FOREBODING
___ 18. SEPTIC
___ 19. TOURNIQUET
___ 20. DISMAY
___ 21. FLUMMOXED
___ 22. PEEVISHLY
___ 23. INFURIATED
___ 24. TRANSFUSION
___ 25. PENCE

A. Perplexed
B. Sarcastic
C. Full of pus
D. The transfer of blood into the bloodstream of somebody who has lost blood
E. Replied in quick response to something someone has said
F. A feeling of dislike
G. Persuaded gently
H. A feeling that something bad is going to happen
I. A course of action to achieve short-term gains
J. A tight band applied around an arm or a leg to stop bleeding
K. Plural of penny
L. Tending to confront and challenge
M. Sources of potential harm
N. Not cautiously
O. Enraged
P. Domineeringly
Q. Irritably
R. Searched thoroughly but handled carelessly
S. A long, bark-covered dwelling place built by some Native North American peoples, esp. the Iroquois
T. Unwilling to cooperate or listen to suggestions
U. Stimulated into great activity
V. Puzzled
W. A thin rod or bar on which meat is pierced for broiling or roasting over a fire
X. Unbelieving
Y. To dishearten, alarm, cause loss of courage

Indian in the Cupboard Vocabulary Matching 4 Answer Key

R - 1. RANSACKED	A.	Perplexed
U - 2. GALVANIZED	B.	Sarcastic
X - 3. INCREDULOUS	C.	Full of pus
I - 4. TACTICS	D.	The transfer of blood into the bloodstream of somebody who has lost blood
S - 5. LONGHOUSE	E.	Replied in quick response to something someone has said
M - 6. PERILS	F.	A feeling of dislike
W - 7. SPIT	G.	Persuaded gently
V - 8. BEMUSED	H.	A feeling that something bad is going to happen
G - 9. COAXED	I.	A course of action to achieve short-term gains
P - 10. IMPERIOUSLY	J.	A tight band applied around an arm or a leg to stop bleeding
F - 11. SCORN	K.	Plural of penny
B - 12. SNIDE	L.	Tending to confront and challenge
T - 13. MULISH	M.	Sources of potential harm
E - 14. RETORTED	N.	Not cautiously
L - 15. DEFIANT	O.	Enraged
N - 16. UNWARILY	P.	Domineeringly
H - 17. FOREBODING	Q.	Irritably
C - 18. SEPTIC	R.	Searched thoroughly but handled carelessly
J - 19. TOURNIQUET	S.	A long, bark-covered dwelling place built by some Native North American peoples, esp. the Iroquois
Y - 20. DISMAY	T.	Unwilling to cooperate or listen to suggestions
A - 21. FLUMMOXED	U.	Stimulated into great activity
Q - 22. PEEVISHLY	V.	Puzzled
O - 23. INFURIATED	W.	A thin rod or bar on which meat is pierced for broiling or roasting over a fire
D - 24. TRANSFUSION	X.	Unbelieving
K - 25. PENCE	Y.	To dishearten, alarm, cause loss of courage

Indian in the Cupboard Vocabulary Magic Squares 1

Match the definition with the vocabulary word. Put your answers in the magic squares below. When your answers are correct, all columns and rows will add to the same number.

A. PERSECUTOR
B. TRUCE
C. FOREBODING
D. DEFIANT
E. VULNERABLE
F. SNIDE
G. RACUOUS
H. INFURIATED
I. MAIZE
J. UNCOMPROMISINGLY
K. SEPTIC
L. PETRIFIED
M. TRANSFUSION
N. SCALPS
O. INTRICATE
P. TRANSFIXED

1. Sarcastic
2. Corn
3. Containing many details or small parts that are skillfully made
4. Tending to confront and challenge
5. The transfer of blood into the bloodstream of somebody who has lost blood
6. An agreed break in any type of dispute or feud
7. Enraged
8. Full of pus
9. A feeling that something bad is going to happen
10. Made motionless
11. Unwilling to back down
12. Open to physical danger or harm
13. Immobile with fear
14. Loud and hoarse or unpleasant-sounding
15. Oppressor; tyrant
16. The skin and hair covering the skulls of enemies; cut off as trophies

A=	B=	C=	D=
E=	F=	G=	H=
I=	J=	K=	L=
M=	N=	O=	P=

Indian in the Cupboard Vocabulary Magic Squares 1 Answer Key

Match the definition with the vocabulary word. Put your answers in the magic squares below. When your answers are correct, all columns and rows will add to the same number.

A. PERSECUTOR
B. TRUCE
C. FOREBODING
D. DEFIANT
E. VULNERABLE
F. SNIDE
G. RACUOUS
H. INFURIATED
I. MAIZE
J. UNCOMPROMISINGLY
K. SEPTIC
L. PETRIFIED
M. TRANSFUSION
N. SCALPS
O. INTRICATE
P. TRANSFIXED

1. Sarcastic
2. Corn
3. Containing many details or small parts that are skillfully made
4. Tending to confront and challenge
5. The transfer of blood into the bloodstream of somebody who has lost blood
6. An agreed break in any type of dispute or feud
7. Enraged
8. Full of pus
9. A feeling that something bad is going to happen
10. Made motionless
11. Unwilling to back down
12. Open to physical danger or harm
13. Immobile with fear
14. Loud and hoarse or unpleasant-sounding
15. Oppressor; tyrant
16. The skin and hair covering the skulls of enemies; cut off as trophies

A=15	B=6	C=9	D=4
E=12	F=1	G=14	H=7
I=2	J=11	K=8	L=13
M=5	N=16	O=3	P=10

Indian in the Cupboard Vocabulary Magic Squares 2

Match the definition with the vocabulary word. Put your answers in the magic squares below. When your answers are correct, all columns and rows will add to the same number.

A. PERILS
B. LONGHOUSE
C. PETRIFIED
D. TETHERED
E. SCORN
F. REGRETFULLY
G. INFURIATED
H. FLUMMOXED
I. OBLIGED
J. TACTICS
K. RAPTURE
L. SPIT
M. TOURNIQUET
N. MAGNANIMOUSLY
O. RESTIVE
P. FOREBODING

1. Perplexed
2. Sources of potential harm
3. A long, bark-covered dwelling place built by some Native North American peoples, esp. the Iroquois
4. Enraged
5. A course of action to achieve short-term gains
6. Having little patience and on the verge of resisting control
7. A feeling that something bad is going to happen
8. Indebted to do something for someone
9. A euphoric state in which somebody is overwhelmed by happiness and unaware of anything else
10. Nobly
11. A tight band applied around an arm or a leg to stop bleeding
12. A thin rod or bar on which meat is pierced for broiling or roasting over a fire
13. A feeling of dislike
14. Tied with a rope or chain
15. Immobile with fear
16. Remorsefully

A=	B=	C=	D=
E=	F=	G=	H=
I=	J=	K=	L=
M=	N=	O=	P=

Indian in the Cupboard Vocabulary Magic Squares 2 Answer Key

Match the definition with the vocabulary word. Put your answers in the magic squares below. When your answers are correct, all columns and rows will add to the same number.

A. PERILS
B. LONGHOUSE
C. PETRIFIED
D. TETHERED
E. SCORN
F. REGRETFULLY
G. INFURIATED
H. FLUMMOXED
I. OBLIGED
J. TACTICS
K. RAPTURE
L. SPIT
M. TOURNIQUET
N. MAGNANIMOUSLY
O. RESTIVE
P. FOREBODING

1. Perplexed
2. Sources of potential harm
3. A long, bark-covered dwelling place built by some Native North American peoples, esp. the Iroquois
4. Enraged
5. A course of action to achieve short-term gains
6. Having little patience and on the verge of resisting control
7. A feeling that something bad is going to happen
8. Indebted to do something for someone
9. A euphoric state in which somebody is overwhelmed by happiness and unaware of anything else
10. Nobly
11. A tight band applied around an arm or a leg to stop bleeding
12. A thin rod or bar on which meat is pierced for broiling or roasting over a fire
13. A feeling of dislike
14. Tied with a rope or chain
15. Immobile with fear
16. Remorsefully

A=2	B=3	C=15	D=14
E=13	F=16	G=4	H=1
I=8	J=5	K=9	L=12
M=11	N=10	O=6	P=7

Indian in the Cupboard Vocabulary Magic Squares 3

Match the definition with the vocabulary word. Put your answers in the magic squares below. When your answers are correct, all columns and rows will add to the same number.

A. BEMUSED
B. SAGEBRUSH
C. INCREDULOUS
D. TRANSFUSION
E. DESPAIR
F. INTRICATE
G. SPIT
H. RAVENOUSLY
I. MINUTE
J. DEFIANT
K. PERILS
L. DISMAY
M. TRANSFIXED
N. IMPERIOUSLY
O. UNWARILY
P. AGHAST

1. Hungrily
2. Made motionless
3. Plant native to North America with silvery wedge-shaped leaves and clusters of small white flowers
4. Sources of potential harm
5. Tending to confront and challenge
6. Unbelieving
7. Overcome with shock
8. A feeling of hopelessness
9. Not cautiously
10. Containing many details or small parts that are skillfully made
11. Extremely small
12. The transfer of blood into the bloodstream of somebody who has lost blood
13. Puzzled
14. To dishearten, alarm, cause loss of courage
15. A thin rod or bar on which meat is pierced for broiling or roasting over a fire
16. Domineeringly

A=	B=	C=	D=
E=	F=	G=	H=
I=	J=	K=	L=
M=	N=	O=	P=

Indian in the Cupboard Vocabulary Magic Squares 3 Answer Key

Match the definition with the vocabulary word. Put your answers in the magic squares below. When your answers are correct, all columns and rows will add to the same number.

A. BEMUSED
B. SAGEBRUSH
C. INCREDULOUS
D. TRANSFUSION
E. DESPAIR
F. INTRICATE
G. SPIT
H. RAVENOUSLY
I. MINUTE
J. DEFIANT
K. PERILS
L. DISMAY
M. TRANSFIXED
N. IMPERIOUSLY
O. UNWARILY
P. AGHAST

1. Hungrily
2. Made motionless
3. Plant native to North America with silvery wedge-shaped leaves and clusters of small white flowers
4. Sources of potential harm
5. Tending to confront and challenge
6. Unbelieving
7. Overcome with shock
8. A feeling of hopelessness
9. Not cautiously
10. Containing many details or small parts that are skillfully made
11. Extremely small
12. The transfer of blood into the bloodstream of somebody who has lost blood
13. Puzzled
14. To dishearten, alarm, cause loss of courage
15. A thin rod or bar on which meat is pierced for broiling or roasting over a fire
16. Domineeringly

A=13	B=3	C=6	D=12
E=8	F=10	G=15	H=1
I=11	J=5	K=4	L=14
M=2	N=16	O=9	P=7

Indian in the Cupboard Vocabulary Magic Squares 4

Match the definition with the vocabulary word. Put your answers in the magic squares below. When your answers are correct, all columns and rows will add to the same number.

A. RELAPSE
B. REGRETFULLY
C. TETHERED
D. FLUMMOXED
E. PENCE
F. RETORTED
G. INFURIATED
H. JOISTS
I. PERILS
J. IMPERIOUSLY
K. BAFFLEMENT
L. INTRICATE
M. RESTIVE
N. GALVANIZED
O. SAGEBRUSH
P. VULNERABLE

1. Plant native to North America with silvery wedge-shaped leaves and clusters of small white flowers
2. Perplexed
3. Domineeringly
4. Plural of penny
5. Sources of potential harm
6. Replied in quick response to something someone has said
7. Open to physical danger or harm
8. Tied with a rope or chain
9. Floor, roof, or ceiling supports
10. Bewilderment
11. To fall ill again after seeming to have made a recovery
12. Stimulated into great activity
13. Remorsefully
14. Having little patience and on the verge of resisting control
15. Enraged
16. Containing many details or small parts that are skillfully made

A=	B=	C=	D=
E=	F=	G=	H=
I=	J=	K=	L=
M=	N=	O=	P=

Indian in the Cupboard Vocabulary Magic Squares 4 Answer Key

Match the definition with the vocabulary word. Put your answers in the magic squares below. When your answers are correct, all columns and rows will add to the same number.

A. RELAPSE
B. REGRETFULLY
C. TETHERED
D. FLUMMOXED
E. PENCE
F. RETORTED
G. INFURIATED
H. JOISTS
I. PERILS
J. IMPERIOUSLY
K. BAFFLEMENT
L. INTRICATE
M. RESTIVE
N. GALVANIZED
O. SAGEBRUSH
P. VULNERABLE

1. Plant native to North America with silvery wedge-shaped leaves and clusters of small white flowers
2. Perplexed
3. Domineeringly
4. Plural of penny
5. Sources of potential harm
6. Replied in quick response to something someone has said
7. Open to physical danger or harm
8. Tied with a rope or chain
9. Floor, roof, or ceiling supports
10. Bewilderment
11. To fall ill again after seeming to have made a recovery
12. Stimulated into great activity
13. Remorsefully
14. Having little patience and on the verge of resisting control
15. Enraged
16. Containing many details or small parts that are skillfully made

A=11	B=13	C=8	D=2
E=4	F=6	G=15	H=9
I=5	J=3	K=10	L=16
M=14	N=12	O=1	P=7

Indian in the Cupboard Vocabulary Word Search 1

```
T R A N S F U S I O N P I M Y R I A D C
C W D C T G D E K C A S N A R A Z B I H
O H P E R S E C U T O R F S D C H G S B
H J N W A A M M R A P T U R E U S I M X
E K S B N P Z C I G T W R T V O L Q A T
R C C Y S P M A G N A N I M O U S L Y J
E H O D F A G H A I U P A N M S D L J P
N T R A I L X I O R S T T S M P E S O J
T Z N Z X L F N B O Z O E Q C H G N I L
R A E P E E G T L T R U D T T A Q K S G
E S C E D D D R I C A R F I H G L V T P
L D T T M S X I G E V N L I D E A P S S
A P E R I L S C E H E I B A E C R P S Z
P J D I U C C A D C N Q R G S N T E E T
S Y I F P C S T N I O U I H P K D M D D
E K N I W S E E J T U E D A A M C I P N
Q C S E D J P H R P S T L S I K Q B S Q
B A N D O L I E R E L D E T R O T E R H
P E E V I S H L Y S Y B E M U S E D Y F
```

A set of leather straps fitted to a horse's head that includes the bit and the reins (6)
A course of action to achieve short-term gains (7)
A euphoric state in which somebody is overwhelmed by happiness and unaware of anything else (7)
A feeling of dislike (5)
A feeling of hopelessness (7)
A kind of belt worn over one shoulder and across the chest (9)
A thin rod or bar on which meat is pierced for broiling or roasting over a fire (4)
A tight band applied around an arm or a leg to stop bleeding (10)
An agreed break in any type of dispute or feud (5)
Bending easily (7)
Containing many details or small parts that are skillfully made (9)
Corn (5)
Devilish (8)
Enraged (10)
Extremely small (6)
Floor, roof, or ceiling supports (6)
Full of pus (6)
Hungrily (10)
Immobile with fear (9)
Indebted to do something for someone (7)
Irritably (9)

Logical (8)
Loud and hoarse or unpleasant-sounding (7)
Made motionless (10)
Nobly (13)
Numerous (6)
Oppressor; tyrant (10)
Overcome with shock (6)
Persuaded gently (6)
Plural of penny (5)
Puzzled (7)
Replied in quick response to something someone has said (8)
Sarcastic (5)
Searched thoroughly but handled carelessly (9)
Shocked (8)
Sources of potential harm (6)
Speaking in a domineering tone (9)
Stared in open-mouthed surprise (5)
Tending to confront and challenge (7)
The skin and hair covering the skulls of enemies; cut off as trophies (6)
The transfer of blood into the bloodstream of somebody who has lost blood (11)
Tied with a rope or chain (8)
To dishearten, alarm, cause loss of courage (6)
To fall ill again after seeming to have made a recovery (7)
Unwilling to cooperate or listen to suggestions (6)

Indian in the Cupboard Vocabulary Word Search 1 Answer Key

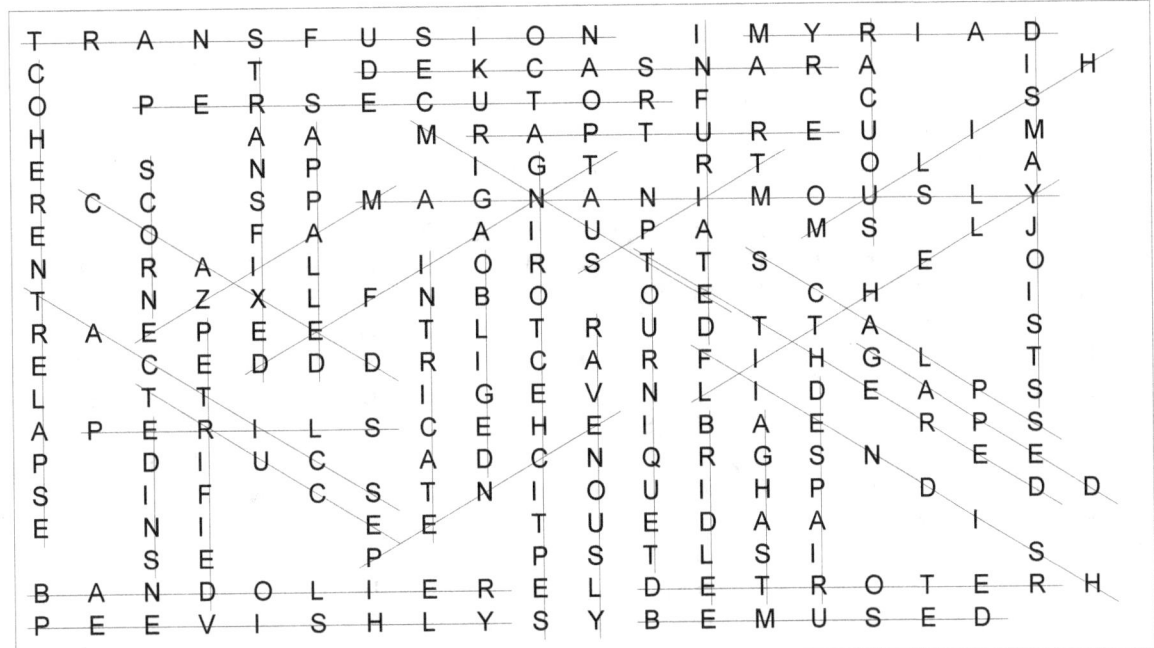

A set of leather straps fitted to a horse's head that includes the bit and the reins (6)
A course of action to achieve short-term gains (7)
A euphoric state in which somebody is overwhelmed by happiness and unaware of anything else (7)
A feeling of dislike (5)
A feeling of hopelessness (7)
A kind of belt worn over one shoulder and across the chest (9)
A thin rod or bar on which meat is pierced for broiling or roasting over a fire (4)
A tight band applied around an arm or a leg to stop bleeding (10)
An agreed break in any type of dispute or feud (5)
Bending easily (7)
Containing many details or small parts that are skillfully made (9)
Corn (5)
Devilish (8)
Enraged (10)
Extremely small (6)
Floor, roof, or ceiling supports (6)
Full of pus (6)
Hungrily (10)
Immobile with fear (9)
Indebted to do something for someone (7)
Irritably (9)
Logical (8)
Loud and hoarse or unpleasant-sounding (7)
Made motionless (10)
Nobly (13)
Numerous (6)
Oppressor; tyrant (10)
Overcome with shock (6)
Persuaded gently (6)
Plural of penny (5)
Puzzled (7)
Replied in quick response to something someone has said (8)
Sarcastic (5)
Searched thoroughly but handled carelessly (9)
Shocked (8)
Sources of potential harm (6)
Speaking in a domineering tone (9)
Stared in open-mouthed surprise (5)
Tending to confront and challenge (7)
The skin and hair covering the skulls of enemies; cut off as trophies (6)
The transfer of blood into the bloodstream of somebody who has lost blood (11)
Tied with a rope or chain (8)
To dishearten, alarm, cause loss of courage (6)
To fall ill again after seeming to have made a recovery (7)
Unwilling to cooperate or listen to suggestions (6)

Indian in the Cupboard Vocabulary Word Search 2

```
H Q R I A P S E D U S M L M I H A C A Z
T S A H G A L V A N I Z E D N S P P E W
A O X C H D I M I W H R E C U P E E S S
C P T R U C E G Y R A T I R R A N E S S
T W B C N X P M M I P F M E E B L C V C
I P R S A I P X R L E E P H D E L I C B
C T E O C N Q U Q Y D E E T U G E O S B
S R C R Z A F U H S S N R L A D B H Q
R A E M S N L S E I U D I T O S I L B
E N T I E D P O T O I O R U T S I Y G
I S R S O G C N S N U S U A S M G L K
L F E N A R V U G S C H S N B I A E I E
O I L S X C T D T C A S L S Z O Y D T D
D X A V M I K E X O R I Y F H J L U H T
N E P B P T G E D R R L J U R X N H E F
A D S S B P X Z D N P U D S K I P J L S
B R E G R E T F U L M Z I M Y Z C Y B
X B E M U S E D D E F Y C O H E R E N T
D                     I A N T M A I Z E
```

A set of leather straps fitted to a horse's head that includes the bit and the reins (6)
A course of action to achieve short-term gains (7)
A feeling of anxiety or fear that something bad is going to occur (12)
A feeling of dislike (5)
A feeling of hopelessness (7)
A kind of belt worn over one shoulder and across the chest (9)
A thin rod or bar on which meat is pierced for broiling or roasting over a fire (4)
A tight band applied around an arm or a leg to stop bleeding (10)
An agreed break in any type of dispute or feud (5)
Bending easily (7)
Corn (5)
Devilish (8)
Domineeringly (11)
Enraged (10)
Extremely small (6)
Floor, roof, or ceiling supports (6)
Full of pus (6)
Indebted to do something for someone (7)
Irritably (9)
Logical (8)
Loud and hoarse or unpleasant-sounding (7)
Made motionless (10)
Not cautiously (8)
Numerous (6)
Oppressor; tyrant (10)
Overcome with shock (6)
Persuaded gently (6)
Plant native to North America with silvery wedge-shaped leaves and clusters of small white flowers (
Plural of penny (5)
Puzzled (7)
Remorsefully (11)
Replied in quick response to something someone has said (8)
Sarcastic (5)
Searched thoroughly but handled carelessly (9)
Shocked (8)
Sources of potential harm (6)
Stared in open-mouthed surprise (5)
Stimulated into great activity (10)
Tending to confront and challenge (7)
The skin and hair covering the skulls of enemies; cut off as trophies (6)
The transfer of blood into the bloodstream of somebody who has lost blood (11)
Tied with a rope or chain (8)
To dishearten, alarm, cause loss of courage (6)
To fall ill again after seeming to have made a recovery (7)
Unbelieving (11)
Unwilling to cooperate or listen to suggestions (6)

Indian in the Cupboard Vocabulary Word Search 2 Answer Key

A set of leather straps fitted to a horse's head that includes the bit and the reins (6)
A course of action to achieve short-term gains (7)
A feeling of anxiety or fear that something bad is going to occur (12)
A feeling of dislike (5)
A feeling of hopelessness (7)
A kind of belt worn over one shoulder and across the chest (9)
A thin rod or bar on which meat is pierced for broiling or roasting over a fire (4)
A tight band applied around an arm or a leg to stop bleeding (10)
An agreed break in any type of dispute or feud (5)
Bending easily (7)
Corn (5)
Devilish (8)
Domineeringly (11)
Enraged (10)
Extremely small (6)
Floor, roof, or ceiling supports (6)
Full of pus (6)
Indebted to do something for someone (7)
Irritably (9)
Logical (8)
Loud and hoarse or unpleasant-sounding (7)
Made motionless (10)
Not cautiously (8)

Numerous (6)
Oppressor; tyrant (10)
Overcome with shock (6)
Persuaded gently (6)
Plant native to North America with silvery wedge-shaped leaves and clusters of small white flowers (
Plural of penny (5)
Puzzled (7)
Remorsefully (11)
Replied in quick response to something someone has said (8)
Sarcastic (5)
Searched thoroughly but handled carelessly (9)
Shocked (8)
Sources of potential harm (6)
Stared in open-mouthed surprise (5)
Stimulated into great activity (10)
Tending to confront and challenge (7)
The skin and hair covering the skulls of enemies; cut off as trophies (6)
The transfer of blood into the bloodstream of somebody who has lost blood (11)
Tied with a rope or chain (8)
To dishearten, alarm, cause loss of courage (6)
To fall ill again after seeming to have made a recovery (7)
Unbelieving (11)
Unwilling to cooperate or listen to suggestions (6)

Indian in the Cupboard Vocabulary Word Search 3

```
X S Y W V R Q V J R W P Y W H M H B S F
Z A M N S T Q O Q V D E F I A N T B U Q
S G P T P K I A F I E N D I S H O Y B B
E E B Z I S G R D D P C Z N D U T T U L
P B T E T H E R E D E E T A C I R T N I
T R C S A T E Z X L S V T R P U S R I J
I U L S O L I D O F U R R C E O M M D
C S T R A N R C M M O C B I C R H A G
R H T P A S Z P M T H R T S F G I G Y
T E S V C V T H U G Q E A I C I Q L W
D L Y R R E C L R N W M B N D A E B S
G A G W X P E N F L O W S U O T L D N
G Q Y D S B H O L C X N L D S E P F
M Q P S R E C R L I N R W I I Q T S
Y H L E M D S I E T S T Q A C D S N K Z
R Q P U D W G P C S Z L G R P O E H G C
I T S W S E N A A V T S Y I S T A J N Y
A E V J D N T K Z I V I V L S N U X J X
D T A I R U F N I R J V Y F Q H R E E
L I T H E L Y Y L L U F T E R G E R E D
```

AGHAST   GAPED   PENCE   RETORTED

BEMUSED   INFURIATED   PERILS   SAGEBRUSH

BRIDLE   INTRICATE   PERSECUTOR   SCALPS

COAXED   JOISTS   PETRIFIED   SCORN

DEFIANT   LITHELY   RACUOUS   SEPTIC

DESPAIR   LONGHOUSE   RAPTURE   SNIDE

DISMAY   MAIZE   RAVENOUSLY   SPIT

FIENDISH   MINUTE   REGRETFULLY   TACTICS

FLUMMOXED   MULISH   RELAPSE   TETHERED

FOREBODING   MYRIAD   RELUCTANT   TRUCE

GALVANIZED   OBLIGED   RESTIVE   UNWARILY

Indian in the Cupboard Vocabulary Word Search 3 Answer Key

AGHAST	GAPED	PENCE	RETORTED
BEMUSED	INFURIATED	PERILS	SAGEBRUSH
BRIDLE	INTRICATE	PERSECUTOR	SCALPS
COAXED	JOISTS	PETRIFIED	SCORN
DEFIANT	LITHELY	RACUOUS	SEPTIC
DESPAIR	LONGHOUSE	RAPTURE	SNIDE
DISMAY	MAIZE	RAVENOUSLY	SPIT
FIENDISH	MINUTE	REGRETFULLY	TACTICS
FLUMMOXED	MULISH	RELAPSE	TETHERED
FOREBODING	MYRIAD	RELUCTANT	TRUCE
GALVANIZED	OBLIGED	RESTIVE	UNWARILY

Indian in the Cupboard Vocabulary Word Search 4

```
H E C T O R I N G J D Y S C O R N S D D K
P D M N O G K Y L E L H C M C A C E I Y
E E R A H B G H L H R I I C C U C K S D
S E I N J L L S J B M T N X C A C M G
P G F N D A I C C P D C U Y O L P A L
A R E S P V J G E B E A T J U P S Y T
I E D P E D O R E H R P V G K S N S F
R T A E F L I C J D E A C M Y H A B D
E E F P W F O S M O X H V I L G I R E F
D V U H V U X T S T H T M I G R F M L
F I L W S G R S N R V E F T A D R G U V
I T L L R E A X A R T R P L Y P A S M
E S Y L E H T I L V U L N P E R A B E X
N E N H N C O H P E C N S N D C V D Y
D R T I U X R T E N R H Y E T H A J E
I F Y L D Y T I R O F M M X W S K N Z Z
S P E N C E E P I U N W A R I L Y I V W
H R N P X G D S L S C O S L C N A Z K
R A P T U R E X S S L C E U T D M W E D T
S A G E B R U S H Y N M Y R I A D D T N
```

AGHAST	GAPED	PENCE	SAGEBRUSH
APPALLED	HECTORING	PERILS	SCALPS
BEMUSED	IMPERIOUSLY	PETRIFIED	SCORN
BRIDLE	JOISTS	RACUOUS	SEPTIC
COAXED	LITHELY	RANSACKED	SNIDE
COHERENT	MAIZE	RAPTURE	SPIT
DEFIANT	MINUTE	RAVENOUSLY	TACTICS
DESPAIR	MULISH	REGRETFULLY	TETHERED
DISMAY	MYRIAD	RELUCTANT	TRUCE
FIENDISH	OBLIGED	RESTIVE	UNWARILY
GALVANIZED	PEEVISHLY	RETORTED	VULNERABLE

Indian in the Cupboard Vocabulary Word Search 4 Answer Key

AGHAST	GAPED	PENCE	SAGEBRUSH
APPALLED	HECTORING	PERILS	SCALPS
BEMUSED	IMPERIOUSLY	PETRIFIED	SCORN
BRIDLE	JOISTS	RACUOUS	SEPTIC
COAXED	LITHELY	RANSACKED	SNIDE
COHERENT	MAIZE	RAPTURE	SPIT
DEFIANT	MINUTE	RAVENOUSLY	TACTICS
DESPAIR	MULISH	REGRETFULLY	TETHERED
DISMAY	MYRIAD	RELUCTANT	TRUCE
FIENDISH	OBLIGED	RESTIVE	UNWARILY
GALVANIZED	PEEVISHLY	RETORTED	VULNERABLE

Indian In The Cupboard Vocabulary Crossword 1

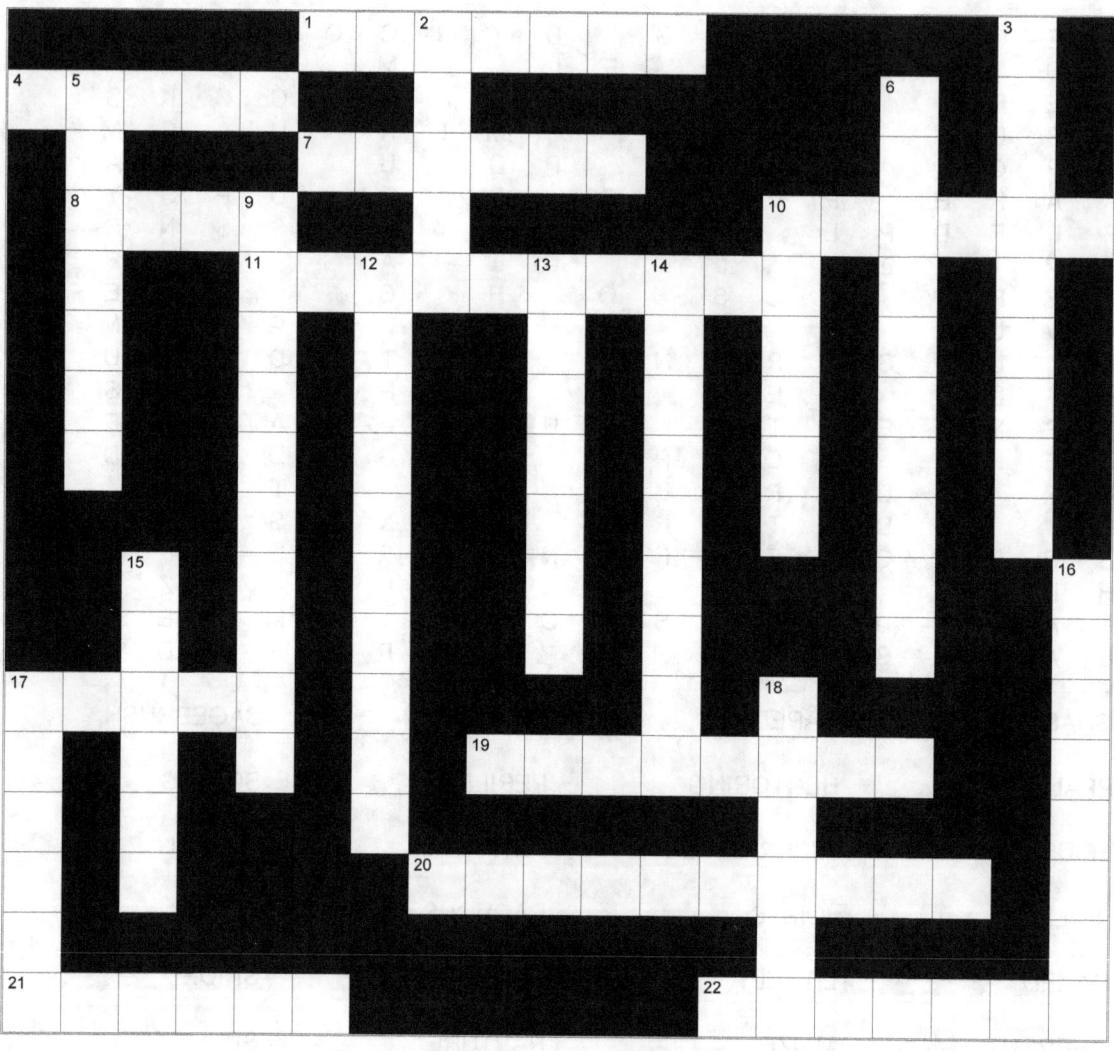

Across
1. A feeling of hopelessness
4. An agreed break in any type of dispute or feud
7. Floor, roof, or ceiling supports
8. A thin rod or bar on which meat is pierced for broiling or roasting over a fire
10. Unwilling to cooperate or listen to suggestions
11. Hungrily
17. Plural of penny
19. Tied with a rope or chain
20. A feeling that something bad is going to happen
21. Full of pus
22. Tending to confront and challenge

Down
2. Sarcastic
3. Searched thoroughly but handled carelessly
5. Having little patience and on the verge of resisting control
6. Stimulated into great activity
9. Made motionless
10. Numerous
12. Open to physical danger or harm
13. Indebted to do something for someone
14. Plant native to North America with silvery wedge-shaped leaves and clusters of small white flowers
15. Extremely small
16. Logical
17. Sources of potential harm
18. A set of leather straps fitted to a horse's head that includes the bit and the reins

Indian In The Cupboard Vocabulary Crossword 1 Answer Key

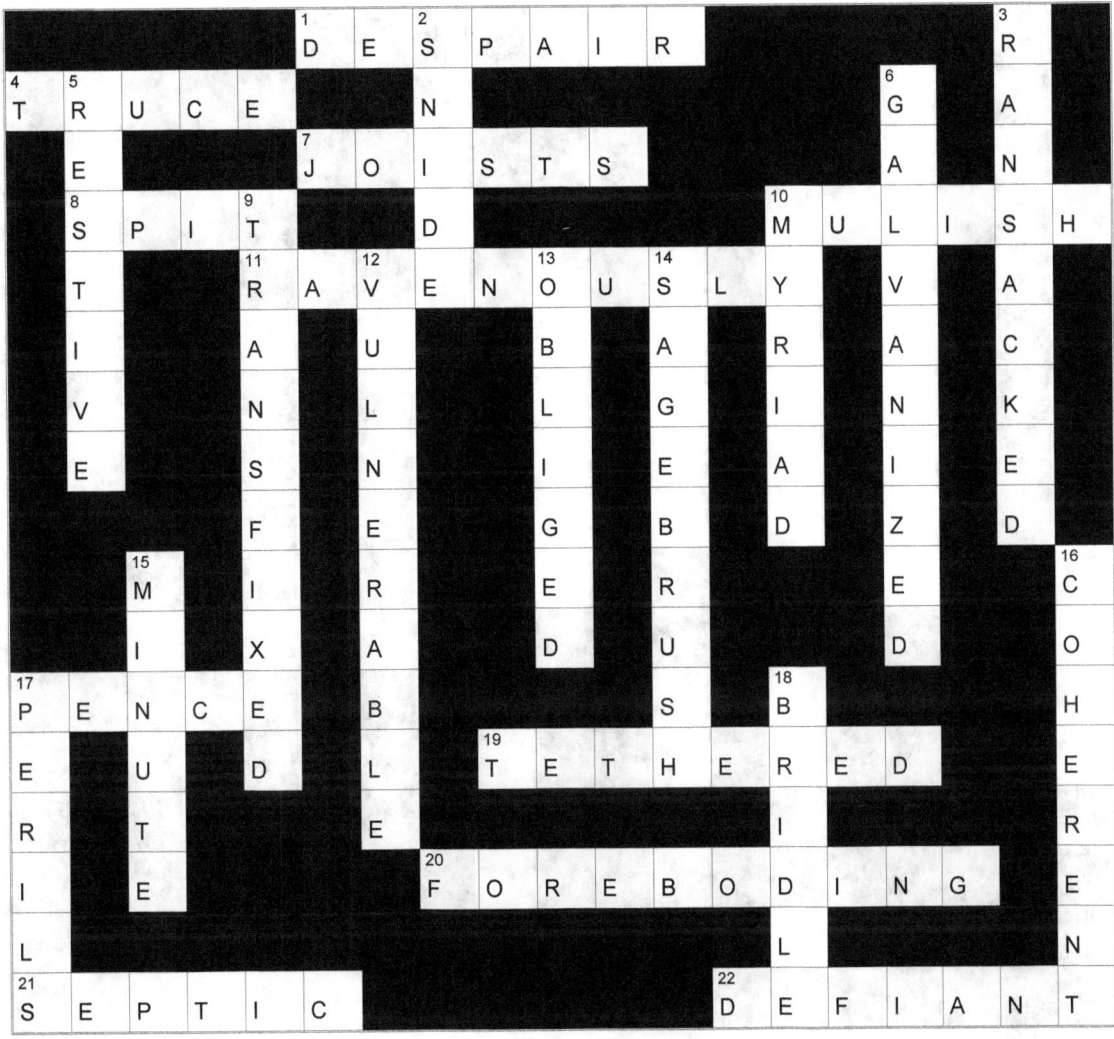

Across
1. A feeling of hopelessness
4. An agreed break in any type of dispute or feud
7. Floor, roof, or ceiling supports
8. A thin rod or bar on which meat is pierced for broiling or roasting over a fire
10. Unwilling to cooperate or listen to suggestions
11. Hungrily
17. Plural of penny
19. Tied with a rope or chain
20. A feeling that something bad is going to happen
21. Full of pus
22. Tending to confront and challenge

Down
2. Sarcastic
3. Searched thoroughly but handled carelessly
5. Having little patience and on the verge of resisting control
6. Stimulated into great activity
9. Made motionless
10. Numerous
12. Open to physical danger or harm
13. Indebted to do something for someone
14. Plant native to North America with silvery wedge-shaped leaves and clusters of small white flowers
15. Extremely small
16. Logical
17. Sources of potential harm
18. A set of leather straps fitted to a horse's head that includes the bit and the reins

Indian In The Cupboard Vocabulary Crossword 2

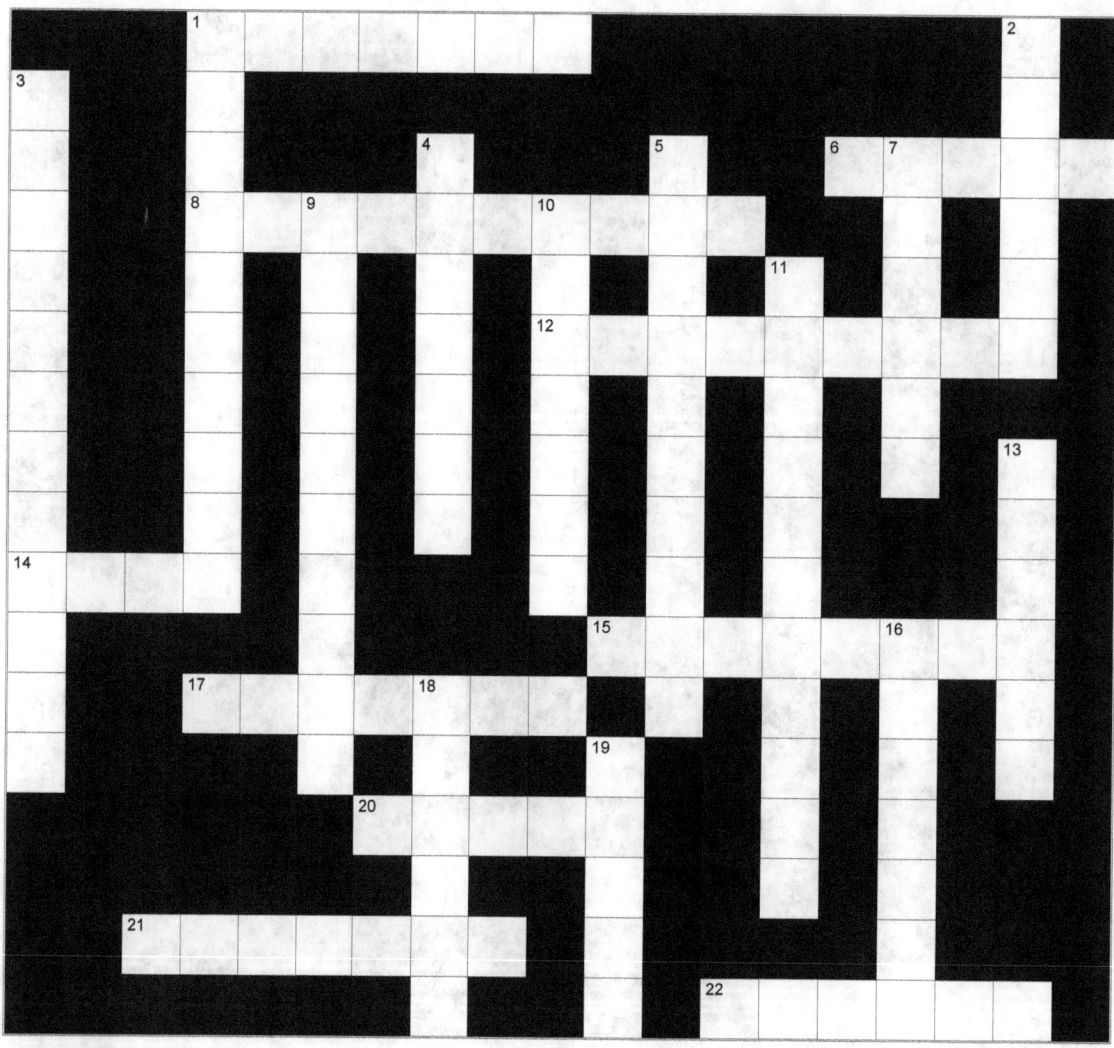

Across
1. Puzzled
6. A feeling of dislike
8. A feeling that something bad is going to happen
12. Perplexed
14. A thin rod or bar on which meat is pierced for broiling or roasting over a fire
15. Replied in quick response to something someone has said
17. To fall ill again after seeming to have made a recovery
20. An agreed break in any type of dispute or feud
21. Bending easily
22. Floor, roof, or ceiling supports

Down
1. Bewilderment
2. Numerous
3. A feeling of anxiety or fear that something bad is going to occur
4. Indebted to do something for someone
5. Enraged
7. Persuaded gently
9. Hungrily
10. Tending to confront and challenge
11. Domineeringly
13. A set of leather straps fitted to a horse's head that includes the bit and the reins
16. A course of action to achieve short-term gains
18. Sources of potential harm
19. Plural of penny

Indian In The Cupboard Vocabulary Crossword 2 Answer Key

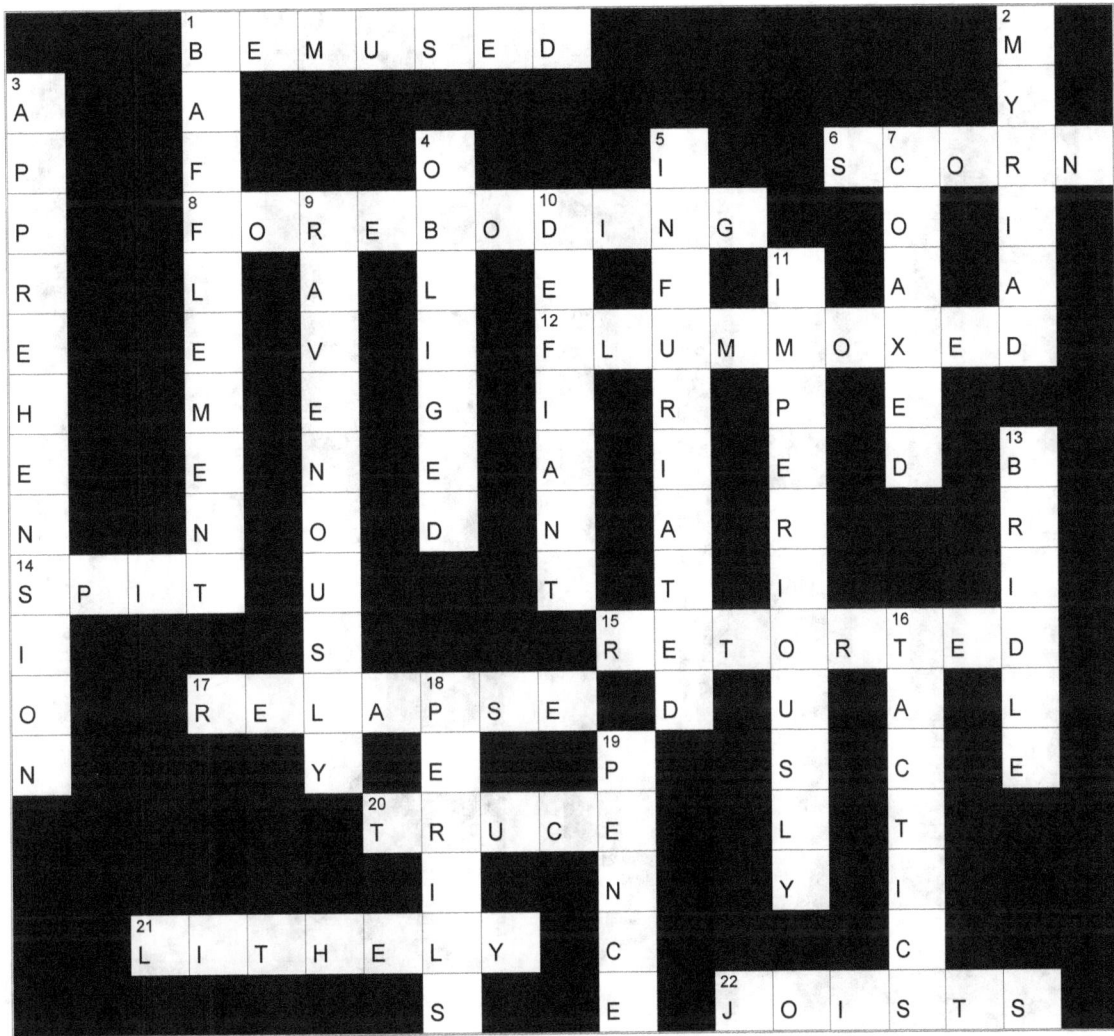

Across
1. Puzzled
6. A feeling of dislike
8. A feeling that something bad is going to happen
12. Perplexed
14. A thin rod or bar on which meat is pierced for broiling or roasting over a fire
15. Replied in quick response to something someone has said
17. To fall ill again after seeming to have made a recovery
20. An agreed break in any type of dispute or feud
21. Bending easily
22. Floor, roof, or ceiling supports

Down
1. Bewilderment
2. Numerous
3. A feeling of anxiety or fear that something bad is going to occur
4. Indebted to do something for someone
5. Enraged
7. Persuaded gently
9. Hungrily
10. Tending to confront and challenge
11. Domineeringly
13. A set of leather straps fitted to a horse's head that includes the bit and the reins
16. A course of action to achieve short-term gains
18. Sources of potential harm
19. Plural of penny

Indian In The Cupboard Vocabulary Crossword 3

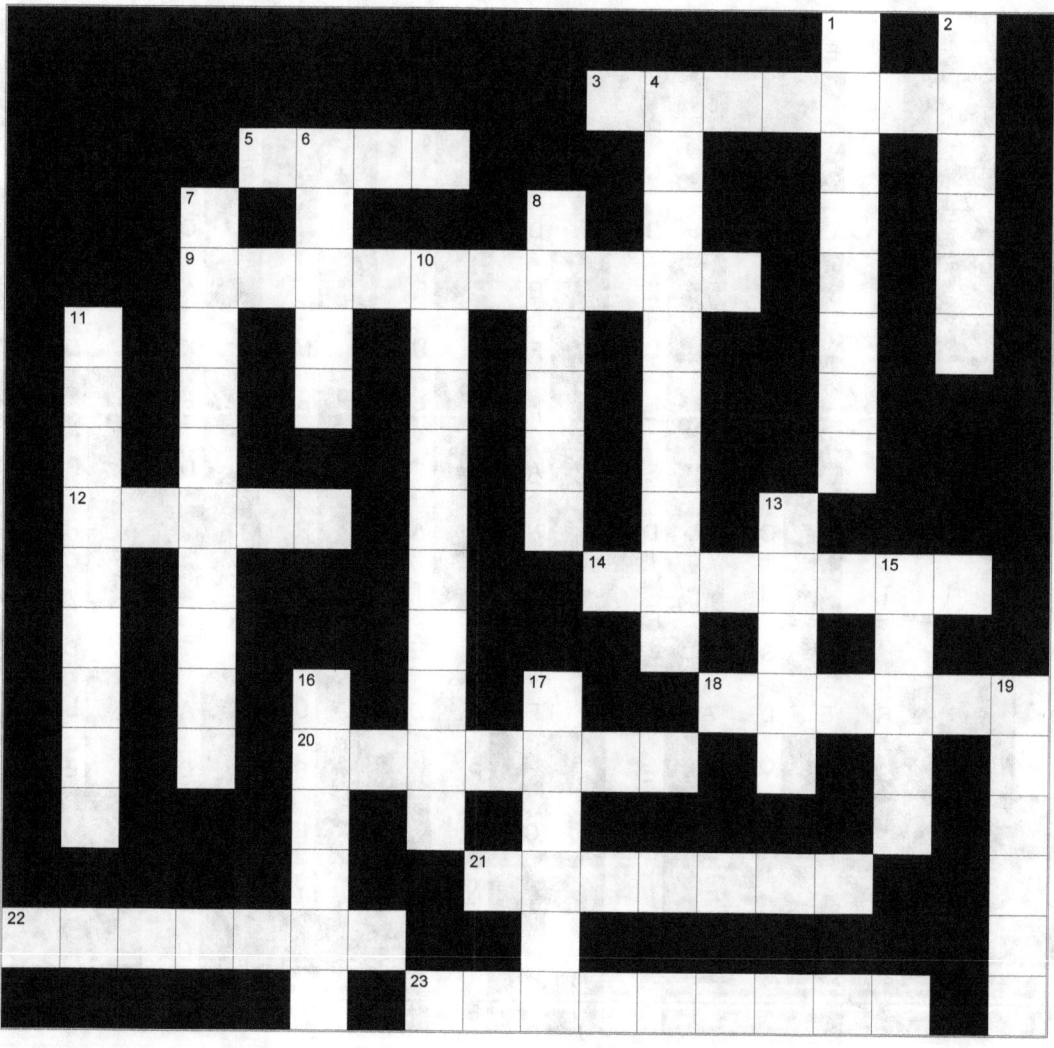

Across
3. Bending easily
5. A thin rod or bar on which meat is pierced for broiling or roasting over a fire
9. Eating any kind of food, including both plants and animals
12. A feeling of dislike
14. To fall ill again after seeming to have made a recovery
18. Sources of potential harm
20. Indebted to do something for someone
21. A course of action to achieve short-term gains
22. Puzzled
23. Containing many details or small parts that are skillfully made

Down
1. Replied in quick response to something someone has said
2. Numerous
4. Enraged
6. Plural of penny
7. A feeling that something bad is going to happen
8. A set of leather straps fitted to a horse's head that includes the bit and the reins
10. Open to physical danger or harm
11. Searched thoroughly but handled carelessly
13. Stared in open-mouthed surprise
15. Sarcastic
16. Persuaded gently
17. Overcome with shock
19. Full of pus

Indian In The Cupboard Vocabulary Crossword 3 Answer Key

Across
3. Bending easily
5. A thin rod or bar on which meat is pierced for broiling or roasting over a fire
9. Eating any kind of food, including both plants and animals
12. A feeling of dislike
14. To fall ill again after seeming to have made a recovery
18. Sources of potential harm
20. Indebted to do something for someone
21. A course of action to achieve short-term gains
22. Puzzled
23. Containing many details or small parts that are skillfully made

Down
1. Replied in quick response to something someone has said
2. Numerous
4. Enraged
6. Plural of penny
7. A feeling that something bad is going to happen
8. A set of leather straps fitted to a horse's head that includes the bit and the reins
10. Open to physical danger or harm
11. Searched thoroughly but handled carelessly
13. Stared in open-mouthed surprise
15. Sarcastic
16. Persuaded gently
17. Overcome with shock
19. Full of pus

Indian In The Cupboard Vocabulary Crossword 4

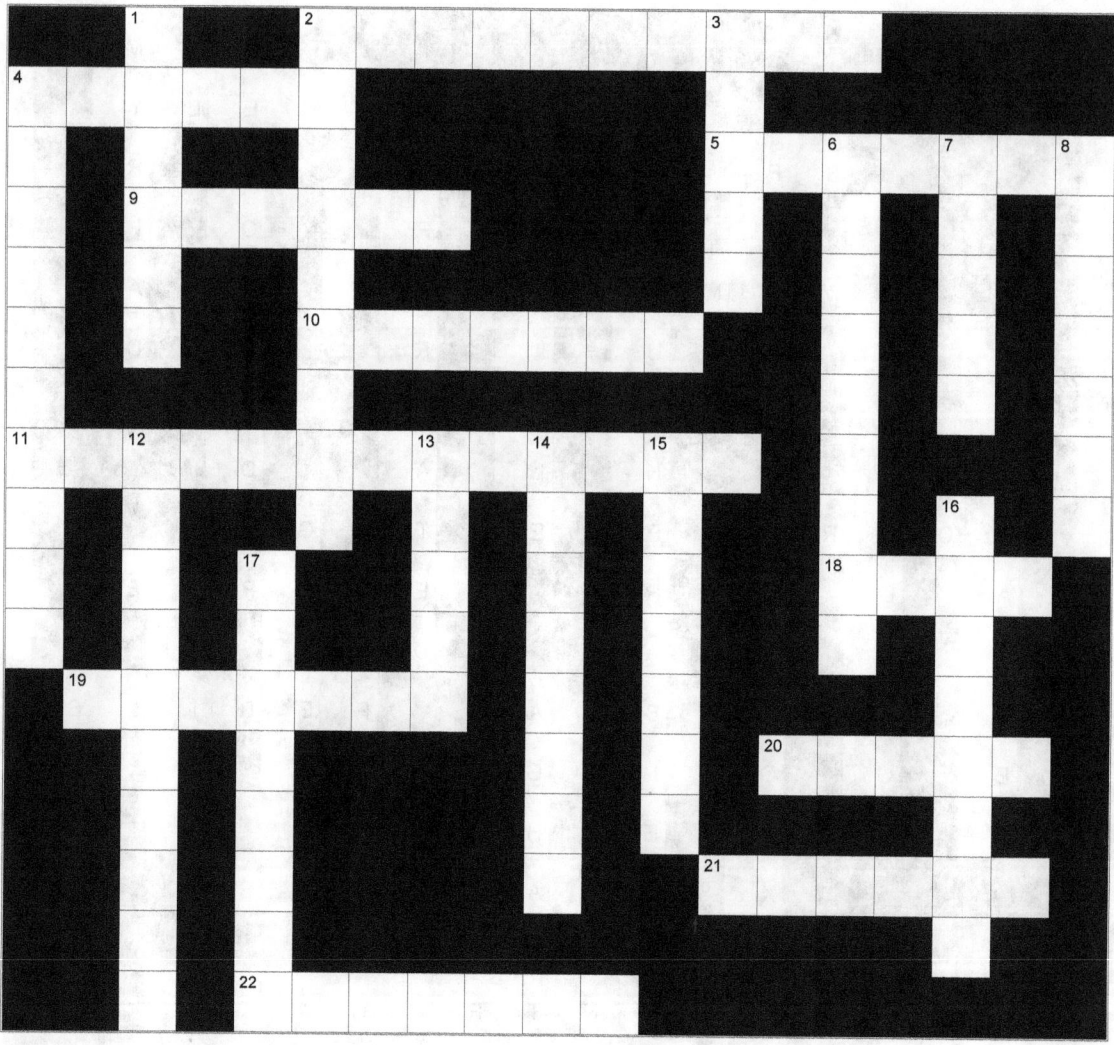

Across
2. Hungrily
4. A set of leather straps fitted to a horse's head that includes the bit and the reins
5. Indebted to do something for someone
9. Extremely small
10. A course of action to achieve short-term gains
11. Nobly
18. A thin rod or bar on which meat is pierced for broiling or roasting over a fire
19. A euphoric state in which somebody is overwhelmed by happiness and unaware of anything else
20. Sarcastic
21. Overcome with shock
22. A feeling of hopelessness

Down
1. To dishearten, alarm, cause loss of courage
2. Hesitant
3. A feeling of dislike
4. Bewilderment
6. A long, bark-covered dwelling place built by some Native North American peoples, esp. the Iroquois
7. Stared in open-mouthed surprise
8. Tending to confront and challenge
12. Stimulated into great activity
13. Corn
14. Not cautiously
15. Bending easily
16. Devilish
17. Tied with a rope or chain

Indian In The Cupboard Vocabulary Crossword 4 Answer Key

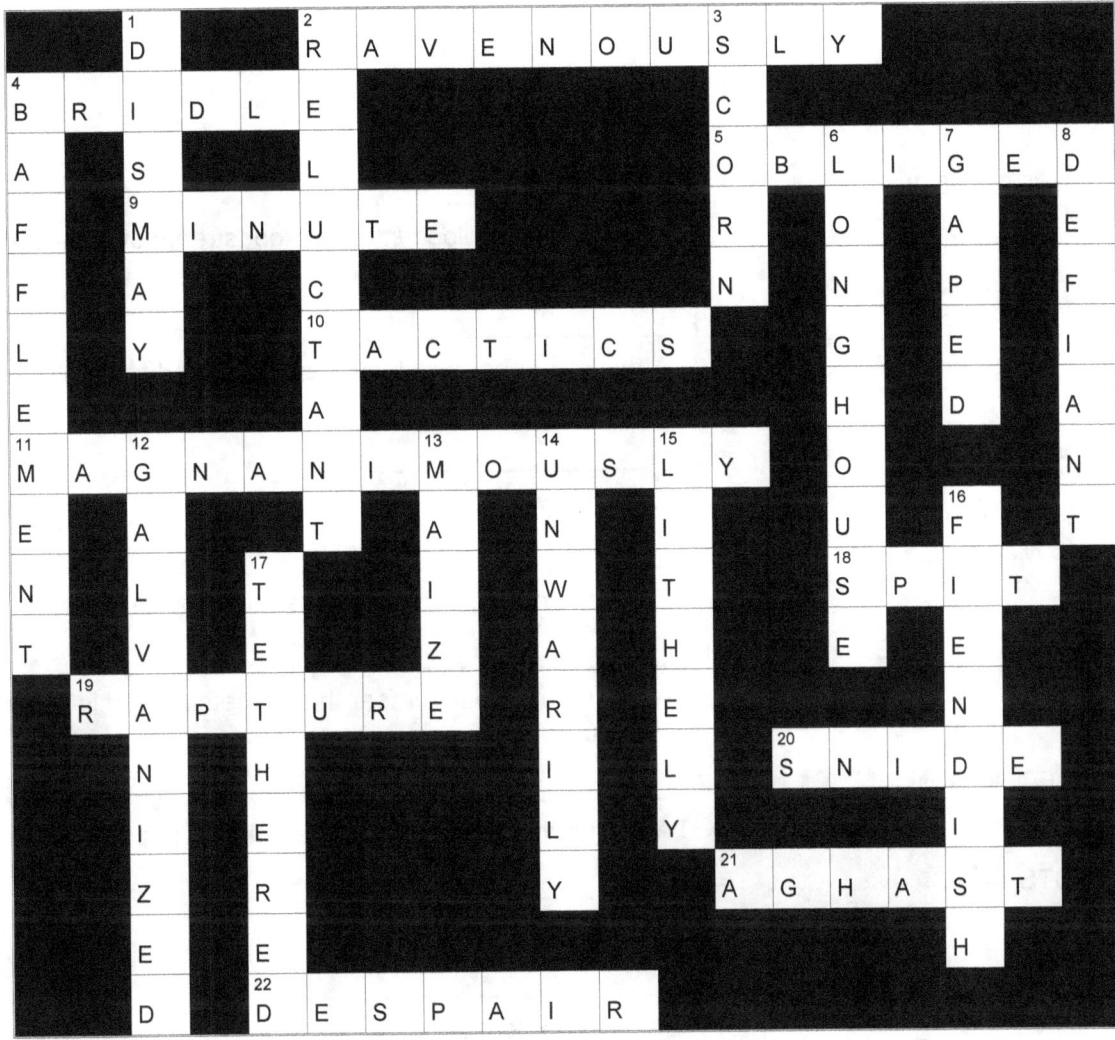

Across
2. Hungrily
4. A set of leather straps fitted to a horse's head that includes the bit and the reins
5. Indebted to do something for someone
9. Extremely small
10. A course of action to achieve short-term gains
11. Nobly
18. A thin rod or bar on which meat is pierced for broiling or roasting over a fire
19. A euphoric state in which somebody is overwhelmed by happiness and unaware of anything else
20. Sarcastic
21. Overcome with shock
22. A feeling of hopelessness

Down
1. To dishearten, alarm, cause loss of courage
2. Hesitant
3. A feeling of dislike
4. Bewilderment
6. A long, bark-covered dwelling place built by some Native North American peoples, esp. the Iroquois
7. Stared in open-mouthed surprise
8. Tending to confront and challenge
12. Stimulated into great activity
13. Corn
14. Not cautiously
15. Bending easily
16. Devilish
17. Tied with a rope or chain

Indian In The Cupboard Vocabulary Juggle Letters 1

1. POIMYRUSILE = 1. _____
Domineeringly

2. ANSFTNIOSRU = 2. _____
The transfer of blood into the bloodstream of somebody who has lost blood

3. PITS = 3. _____
A thin rod or bar on which meat is pierced for broiling or roasting over a fire

4. ZMIAE = 4. _____
Corn

5. AISYDM = 5. _____
To dishearten, alarm, cause loss of courage

6. NEOPRSIHPNAE = 6. _____
A feeling of anxiety or fear that something bad is going to occur

7. BDEOOGFRIN = 7. _____
A feeling that something bad is going to happen

8. HGTSAA = 8. _____
Overcome with shock

9. XEODAC = 9. _____
Persuaded gently

10. BEUNRLLEAV =10. _____
Open to physical danger or harm

11. USPCRETEOR =11. _____
Oppressor; tyrant

12. DIESN =12. _____
Sarcastic

13. UQONETTURI =13. _____
A tight band applied around an arm or a leg to stop bleeding

14. EMTBNFEFAL =14. _____
Bewilderment

Indian In The Cupboard Vocabulary Juggle Letters 1 Answer Key

1. POIMYRUSILE = 1. IMPERIOUSLY
   Domineeringly

2. ANSFTNIOSRU = 2. TRANSFUSION
   The transfer of blood into the bloodstream of somebody who has lost blood

3. PITS = 3. SPIT
   A thin rod or bar on which meat is pierced for broiling or roasting over a fire

4. ZMIAE = 4. MAIZE
   Corn

5. AISYDM = 5. DISMAY
   To dishearten, alarm, cause loss of courage

6. NEOPRSIHPNAE = 6. APPREHENSION
   A feeling of anxiety or fear that something bad is going to occur

7. BDEOOGFRIN = 7. FOREBODING
   A feeling that something bad is going to happen

8. HGTSAA = 8. AGHAST
   Overcome with shock

9. XEODAC = 9. COAXED
   Persuaded gently

10. BEUNRLLEAV = 10. VULNERABLE
    Open to physical danger or harm

11. USPCRETEOR = 11. PERSECUTOR
    Oppressor; tyrant

12. DIESN = 12. SNIDE
    Sarcastic

13. UQONETTURI = 13. TOURNIQUET
    A tight band applied around an arm or a leg to stop bleeding

14. EMTBNFEFAL = 14. BAFFLEMENT
    Bewilderment

Indian In The Cupboard Vocabulary Juggle Letters 2

1. BAHSERGUS = 1. _____
Plant native to North America with silvery wedge-shaped leaves and clusters of small white flowers

2. MSUEBDE = 2. _____
Puzzled

3. EDHINSIF = 3. _____
Devilish

4. RUWNIYAL = 4. _____
Not cautiously

5. NSDIE = 5. _____
Sarcastic

6. EDEEHTTR = 6. _____
Tied with a rope or chain

7. ENCEP = 7. _____
Plural of penny

8. ELRIBD = 8. _____
A set of leather straps fitted to a horse's head that includes the bit and the reins

9. IPEEFITDR = 9. _____
Immobile with fear

10. RTQIOUTUEN =10. _____
A tight band applied around an arm or a leg to stop bleeding

11. APURETR =11. _____
A euphoric state in which somebody is overwhelmed by happiness and unaware of anything else

12. HUIMLS =12. _____
Unwilling to cooperate or listen to suggestions

13. RPEESIOAPNNH =13. _____
A feeling of anxiety or fear that something bad is going to occur

14. EMFEAFTLBN =14. _____
Bewilderment

Indian In The Cupboard Vocabulary Juggle Letters 2 Answer Key

1. BAHSERGUS = 1. SAGEBRUSH
   Plant native to North America with silvery wedge-shaped leaves and clusters of small white flowers

2. MSUEBDE = 2. BEMUSED
   Puzzled

3. EDHINSIF = 3. FIENDISH
   Devilish

4. RUWNIYAL = 4. UNWARILY
   Not cautiously

5. NSDIE = 5. SNIDE
   Sarcastic

6. EDEEHTTR = 6. TETHERED
   Tied with a rope or chain

7. ENCEP = 7. PENCE
   Plural of penny

8. ELRIBD = 8. BRIDLE
   A set of leather straps fitted to a horse's head that includes the bit and the reins

9. IPEEFITDR = 9. PETRIFIED
   Immobile with fear

10. RTQIOUTUEN =10. TOURNIQUET
    A tight band applied around an arm or a leg to stop bleeding

11. APURETR =11. RAPTURE
    A euphoric state in which somebody is overwhelmed by happiness and unaware of anything else

12. HUIMLS =12. MULISH
    Unwilling to cooperate or listen to suggestions

13. RPEESIOAPNNH =13. APPREHENSION
    A feeling of anxiety or fear that something bad is going to occur

14. EMFEAFTLBN =14. BAFFLEMENT
    Bewilderment

Indian In The Cupboard Vocabulary Juggle Letters 3

1. GIREHTCON = 1. _____
   Speaking in a domineering tone

2. ILERSP = 2. _____
   Sources of potential harm

3. MSYADI = 3. _____
   To dishearten, alarm, cause loss of courage

4. INRYWULA = 4. _____
   Not cautiously

5. INOEFGBORD = 5. _____
   A feeling that something bad is going to happen

6. TEHOECRN = 6. _____
   Logical

7. HREETETD = 7. _____
   Tied with a rope or chain

8. IENTUM = 8. _____
   Extremely small

9. NOGOLPYUMRCISINM = 9. _____
   Unwilling to back down

10. HGATSA =10. _____
    Overcome with shock

11. OEERTDRT =11. _____
    Replied in quick response to something someone has said

12. EGPDA =12. _____
    Stared in open-mouthed surprise

13. ROIMUOOSVN =13. _____
    Eating any kind of food, including both plants and animals

14. ADEKNSCRA =14. _____
    Searched thoroughly but handled carelessly

Indian In The Cupboard Vocabulary Juggle Letters 3 Answer Key

1. GIREHTCON = 1. HECTORING
Speaking in a domineering tone

2. ILERSP = 2. PERILS
Sources of potential harm

3. MSYADI = 3. DISMAY
To dishearten, alarm, cause loss of courage

4. INRYWULA = 4. UNWARILY
Not cautiously

5. INOEFGBORD = 5. FOREBODING
A feeling that something bad is going to happen

6. TEHOECRN = 6. COHERENT
Logical

7. HREETETD = 7. TETHERED
Tied with a rope or chain

8. IENTUM = 8. MINUTE
Extremely small

9. NOGOLPYUMRCISINM = 9. UNCOMPROMISINGLY
Unwilling to back down

10. HGATSA = 10. AGHAST
Overcome with shock

11. OEERTDRT = 11. RETORTED
Replied in quick response to something someone has said

12. EGPDA = 12. GAPED
Stared in open-mouthed surprise

13. ROIMUOOSVN = 13. OMNIVOROUS
Eating any kind of food, including both plants and animals

14. ADEKNSCRA = 14. RANSACKED
Searched thoroughly but handled carelessly

Indian In The Cupboard Vocabulary Juggle Letters 4

1. INUOUQTRET = 1. _____
A tight band applied around an arm or a leg to stop bleeding

2. DOLEIGB = 2. _____
Indebted to do something for someone

3. SOJTSI = 3. _____
Floor, roof, or ceiling supports

4. RYMIAD = 4. _____
Numerous

5. IAYMDS = 5. _____
To dishearten, alarm, cause loss of courage

6. EAPRDIS = 6. _____
A feeling of hopelessness

7. IIERTCATN = 7. _____
Containing many details or small parts that are skillfully made

8. OEHUNOSLG = 8. _____
A long, bark-covered dwelling place built by some Native North American peoples, esp. the Iroquois

9. OPGMRLIUONCYMNSI = 9. _____
Unwilling to back down

10. ILSUMH =10. _____
Unwilling to cooperate or listen to suggestions

11. UDSBEEM =11. _____
Puzzled

12. RETEDOTR =12. _____
Replied in quick response to something someone has said

13. ASREELP =13. _____
To fall ill again after seeming to have made a recovery

14. PGAED =14. _____
Stared in open-mouthed surprise

Copyrighted

Indian In The Cupboard Vocabulary Juggle Letters 4 Answer Key

1. INUOUQTRET = 1. TOURNIQUET
   A tight band applied around an arm or a leg to stop bleeding

2. DOLEIGB = 2. OBLIGED
   Indebted to do something for someone

3. SOJTSI = 3. JOISTS
   Floor, roof, or ceiling supports

4. RYMIAD = 4. MYRIAD
   Numerous

5. IAYMDS = 5. DISMAY
   To dishearten, alarm, cause loss of courage

6. EAPRDIS = 6. DESPAIR
   A feeling of hopelessness

7. IIERTCATN = 7. INTRICATE
   Containing many details or small parts that are skillfully made

8. OEHUNOSLG = 8. LONGHOUSE
   A long, bark-covered dwelling place built by some Native North American peoples, esp. the Iroquois

9. OPGMRLIUONCYMNSI = 9. UNCOMPROMISINGLY
   Unwilling to back down

10. ILSUMH =10. MULISH
    Unwilling to cooperate or listen to suggestions

11. UDSBEEM =11. BEMUSED
    Puzzled

12. RETEDOTR =12. RETORTED
    Replied in quick response to something someone has said

13. ASREELP =13. RELAPSE
    To fall ill again after seeming to have made a recovery

14. PGAED =14. GAPED
    Stared in open-mouthed surprise

AGHAST	Overcome with shock
APPALLED	Shocked
APPREHENSION	A feeling of anxiety or fear that something bad is going to occur
BAFFLEMENT	Bewilderment
BANDOLIER	A kind of belt worn over one shoulder and across the chest
BEMUSED	Puzzled

BRIDLE	A set of leather straps fitted to a horse's head that includes the bit and the reins
COAXED	Persuaded gently
COHERENT	Logical
DEFIANT	Tending to confront and challenge
DESPAIR	A feeling of hopelessness
DISMAY	To dishearten, alarm, cause loss of courage

FIENDISH	Devilish
FLUMMOXED	Perplexed
FOREBODING	A feeling that something bad is going to happen
GALVANIZED	Stimulated into great activity
GAPED	Stared in open-mouthed surprise
HECTORING	Speaking in a domineering tone

IMPERIOUSLY	Domineeringly
INCREDULOUS	Unbelieving
INFURIATED	Enraged
INTRICATE	Containing many details or small parts that are skillfully made
JOISTS	Floor, roof, or ceiling supports
LITHELY	Bending easily

LONGHOUSE	A long, bark-covered dwelling place built by some Native North American peoples, esp. the Iroquois
MAGNANIMOUSLY	Nobly
MAIZE	Corn
MINUTE	Extremely small
MULISH	Unwilling to cooperate or listen to suggestions
MYRIAD	Numerous

OBLIGED	Indebted to do something for someone
OMNIVOROUS	Eating any kind of food, including both plants and animals
PEEVISHLY	Irritably
PENCE	Plural of penny
PERILS	Sources of potential harm
PERSECUTOR	Oppressor; tyrant

PETRIFIED	Immobile with fear
RACUOUS	Loud and hoarse or unpleasant-sounding
RANSACKED	Searched thoroughly but handled carelessly
RAPTURE	A euphoric state in which somebody is overwhelmed by happiness
RAVENOUSLY	Hungrily
REGRETFULLY	Remorsefully

RELAPSE	To fall ill again after seeming to have made a recovery
RELUCTANT	Hesitant
RESTIVE	Having little patience and on the verge of resisting control
RETORTED	Replied in quick response to something someone has said
SAGEBRUSH	Plant native to North America with silvery wedge-shaped leaves and clusters of small white flowers
SCALPS	The skin and hair covering the skulls of enemies; cut off as trophies

SCORN	A feeling of dislike
SEPTIC	Full of pus
SNIDE	Sarcastic
SPIT	A thin rod or bar on which meat is pierced for broiling or roasting over a fire
TACTICS	A course of action to achieve short-term gains
TETHERED	Tied with a rope or chain

TOURNIQUET	A tight band applied around an arm or a leg to stop bleeding
TRANSFIXED	Made motionless
TRANSFUSION	The transfer of blood into the bloodstream of somebody who has lost blood
TRUCE	An agreed break in any type of dispute or feud
UNCOMPROMISINGLY	Unwilling to back down
UNWARILY	Not cautiously

VULNERABLE	Open to physical danger or harm

Indian In The Cupboard Vocab

SPIT	OBLIGED	DEFIANT	MULISH	MAIZE
TRUCE	TETHERED	PEEVISHLY	COAXED	RELAPSE
TACTICS	FLUMMOXED	FREE SPACE	INTRICATE	INFURIATED
SEPTIC	OMNIVOROUS	RESTIVE	LONGHOUSE	RETORTED
RACUOUS	RANSACKED	PENCE	APPALLED	SCORN

Indian In The Cupboard Vocab

SAGEBRUSH	PERILS	GAPED	RAVENOUSLY	TOURNIQUET
IMPERIOUSLY	PERSECUTOR	GALVANIZED	APPREHENSION	REGRETFULLY
BAFFLEMENT	RAPTURE	FREE SPACE	TRANSFIXED	TRANSFUSION
LITHELY	SNIDE	BRIDLE	SCALPS	DESPAIR
MAGNANIMOUSLY	JOISTS	BEMUSED	VULNERABLE	BANDOLIER

Indian In The Cupboard Vocab

GAPED	SPIT	BAFFLEMENT	OBLIGED	DESPAIR
RAVENOUSLY	FOREBODING	PEEVISHLY	SCALPS	LONGHOUSE
SCORN	MAIZE	FREE SPACE	TETHERED	SNIDE
MULISH	REGRETFULLY	LITHELY	PERILS	RELUCTANT
APPALLED	BANDOLIER	RACUOUS	UNWARILY	RESTIVE

Indian In The Cupboard Vocab

GALVANIZED	SAGEBRUSH	JOISTS	RAPTURE	TRUCE
MINUTE	TOURNIQUET	BRIDLE	SEPTIC	MYRIAD
DEFIANT	IMPERIOUSLY	FREE SPACE	RANSACKED	RETORTED
FLUMMOXED	VULNERABLE	PETRIFIED	FIENDISH	PERSECUTOR
INFURIATED	TACTICS	INTRICATE	TRANSFUSION	APPREHENSION

Indian In The Cupboard Vocab

SNIDE	LONGHOUSE	TACTICS	MYRIAD	PETRIFIED
RELUCTANT	FLUMMOXED	UNWARILY	OMNIVOROUS	OBLIGED
INCREDULOUS	BAFFLEMENT	FREE SPACE	RESTIVE	JOISTS
MINUTE	LITHELY	SCORN	MULISH	GAPED
TETHERED	TRANSFIXED	BEMUSED	PEEVISHLY	MAIZE

Indian In The Cupboard Vocab

DESPAIR	APPALLED	DISMAY	BANDOLIER	TRUCE
SPIT	BRIDLE	TOURNIQUET	APPREHENSION	INTRICATE
SCALPS	RAPTURE	FREE SPACE	TRANSFUSION	FOREBODING
RAVENOUSLY	RACUOUS	DEFIANT	IMPERIOUSLY	INFURIATED
FIENDISH	RETORTED	HECTORING	COHERENT	VULNERABLE

Indian In The Cupboard Vocab

COAXED	TRANSFIXED	FIENDISH	PEEVISHLY	PENCE
RAPTURE	TRUCE	SEPTIC	IMPERIOUSLY	BAFFLEMENT
REGRETFULLY	INFURIATED	FREE SPACE	VULNERABLE	FOREBODING
INCREDULOUS	MAGNANIMOUSLY	RACUOUS	BRIDLE	BANDOLIER
MAIZE	COHERENT	LITHELY	DISMAY	JOISTS

Indian In The Cupboard Vocab

RELAPSE	SCALPS	RELUCTANT	MYRIAD	AGHAST
TACTICS	SPIT	DESPAIR	DEFIANT	UNWARILY
FLUMMOXED	PERSECUTOR	FREE SPACE	BEMUSED	GAPED
OBLIGED	TETHERED	MINUTE	TRANSFUSION	RAVENOUSLY
RESTIVE	TOURNIQUET	SNIDE	INTRICATE	SCORN

Indian In The Cupboard Vocab

MULISH	REGRETFULLY	RESTIVE	PENCE	COAXED
PETRIFIED	RELUCTANT	OMNIVOROUS	GALVANIZED	AGHAST
FOREBODING	RANSACKED	FREE SPACE	DESPAIR	SNIDE
PERSECUTOR	COHERENT	BRIDLE	RELAPSE	RAPTURE
MYRIAD	DISMAY	TOURNIQUET	RACUOUS	PERILS

Indian In The Cupboard Vocab

MINUTE	LONGHOUSE	RETORTED	SEPTIC	TRANSFIXED
BANDOLIER	VULNERABLE	APPREHENSION	BEMUSED	TETHERED
INCREDULOUS	INFURIATED	FREE SPACE	APPALLED	SCALPS
MAIZE	TRUCE	TRANSFUSION	TACTICS	SAGEBRUSH
UNWARILY	HECTORING	SCORN	INTRICATE	PEEVISHLY

Indian In The Cupboard Vocab

DESPAIR	APPREHENSION	TETHERED	BEMUSED	RACUOUS
APPALLED	MULISH	VULNERABLE	PETRIFIED	MINUTE
COHERENT	SCALPS	FREE SPACE	HECTORING	JOISTS
IMPERIOUSLY	FLUMMOXED	PEEVISHLY	TRANSFUSION	COAXED
FOREBODING	GAPED	INCREDULOUS	MAIZE	INTRICATE

Indian In The Cupboard Vocab

PENCE	RESTIVE	SEPTIC	OBLIGED	PERSECUTOR
BAFFLEMENT	LONGHOUSE	RAPTURE	TRUCE	SNIDE
RELAPSE	REGRETFULLY	FREE SPACE	BRIDLE	RELUCTANT
MYRIAD	SCORN	MAGNANIMOUSLY	RETORTED	RAVENOUSLY
LITHELY	UNWARILY	INFURIATED	PERILS	SAGEBRUSH

Indian In The Cupboard Vocab

OBLIGED	LITHELY	SCALPS	MULISH	PETRIFIED
GALVANIZED	GAPED	AGHAST	DEFIANT	INTRICATE
FLUMMOXED	IMPERIOUSLY	FREE SPACE	RESTIVE	RELAPSE
SPIT	COAXED	UNWARILY	APPREHENSION	TACTICS
JOISTS	COHERENT	MYRIAD	RANSACKED	RACUOUS

Indian In The Cupboard Vocab

TETHERED	LONGHOUSE	BRIDLE	REGRETFULLY	DESPAIR
HECTORING	BANDOLIER	OMNIVOROUS	TOURNIQUET	MAGNANIMOUSLY
PENCE	SAGEBRUSH	FREE SPACE	RAVENOUSLY	DISMAY
RELUCTANT	PERSECUTOR	MINUTE	SNIDE	PERILS
BEMUSED	TRANSFIXED	APPALLED	TRUCE	BAFFLEMENT

Indian In The Cupboard Vocab

TETHERED	JOISTS	SCORN	COHERENT	INFURIATED
DISMAY	MAGNANIMOUSLY	TOURNIQUET	IMPERIOUSLY	UNWARILY
OBLIGED	SAGEBRUSH	FREE SPACE	INTRICATE	RAPTURE
SEPTIC	MULISH	TACTICS	RAVENOUSLY	FLUMMOXED
RELUCTANT	RANSACKED	OMNIVOROUS	SNIDE	PERILS

Indian In The Cupboard Vocab

DESPAIR	MAIZE	GAPED	BAFFLEMENT	BEMUSED
PEEVISHLY	RETORTED	MYRIAD	BANDOLIER	SCALPS
REGRETFULLY	HECTORING	FREE SPACE	APPALLED	SPIT
DEFIANT	TRANSFIXED	MINUTE	LONGHOUSE	RESTIVE
PENCE	FOREBODING	AGHAST	LITHELY	GALVANIZED

Indian In The Cupboard Vocab

INCREDULOUS	BANDOLIER	RETORTED	SEPTIC	OBLIGED
LONGHOUSE	PERILS	BAFFLEMENT	GALVANIZED	DISMAY
RELAPSE	JOISTS	FREE SPACE	MYRIAD	LITHELY
RAVENOUSLY	DESPAIR	RANSACKED	APPREHENSION	PETRIFIED
UNWARILY	IMPERIOUSLY	PEEVISHLY	TRANSFUSION	RAPTURE

Indian In The Cupboard Vocab

SNIDE	FLUMMOXED	MAGNANIMOUSLY	RACUOUS	VULNERABLE
RESTIVE	BRIDLE	OMNIVOROUS	MULISH	MINUTE
TRANSFIXED	COHERENT	FREE SPACE	INTRICATE	COAXED
PERSECUTOR	REGRETFULLY	MAIZE	APPALLED	PENCE
BEMUSED	TRUCE	FIENDISH	HECTORING	GAPED

Indian In The Cupboard Vocab

RESTIVE	TOURNIQUET	SAGEBRUSH	MINUTE	BANDOLIER
TRUCE	AGHAST	MAIZE	PETRIFIED	REGRETFULLY
JOISTS	LONGHOUSE	FREE SPACE	SCALPS	DISMAY
TETHERED	SEPTIC	PENCE	RELUCTANT	VULNERABLE
BRIDLE	INTRICATE	MYRIAD	PEEVISHLY	TRANSFIXED

Indian In The Cupboard Vocab

RACUOUS	LITHELY	SCORN	PERILS	FOREBODING
COAXED	INFURIATED	APPREHENSION	RAPTURE	DESPAIR
HECTORING	DEFIANT	FREE SPACE	PERSECUTOR	UNWARILY
RANSACKED	OBLIGED	MAGNANIMOUSLY	SPIT	BAFFLEMENT
RELAPSE	FLUMMOXED	GALVANIZED	MULISH	SNIDE

Indian In The Cupboard Vocab

APPREHENSION	RAVENOUSLY	JOISTS	APPALLED	RANSACKED
AGHAST	FLUMMOXED	PEEVISHLY	BANDOLIER	RACUOUS
COHERENT	PETRIFIED	FREE SPACE	RELAPSE	VULNERABLE
SCORN	REGRETFULLY	TETHERED	HECTORING	DISMAY
PENCE	OBLIGED	BAFFLEMENT	BRIDLE	MINUTE

Indian In The Cupboard Vocab

PERSECUTOR	TRANSFUSION	DESPAIR	GAPED	INTRICATE
PERILS	SAGEBRUSH	COAXED	MYRIAD	FIENDISH
MAIZE	TOURNIQUET	FREE SPACE	TACTICS	OMNIVOROUS
SEPTIC	SNIDE	RESTIVE	FOREBODING	TRANSFIXED
DEFIANT	LITHELY	MAGNANIMOUSLY	SPIT	INFURIATED

Indian In The Cupboard Vocab

APPALLED	HECTORING	FIENDISH	TOURNIQUET	REGRETFULLY
LITHELY	TACTICS	AGHAST	COHERENT	APPREHENSION
UNWARILY	RELAPSE	FREE SPACE	SNIDE	RELUCTANT
RANSACKED	PERILS	LONGHOUSE	PETRIFIED	GAPED
BAFFLEMENT	DESPAIR	MINUTE	RAVENOUSLY	RETORTED

Indian In The Cupboard Vocab

PEEVISHLY	BEMUSED	OMNIVOROUS	INCREDULOUS	OBLIGED
VULNERABLE	BANDOLIER	TRUCE	TRANSFIXED	JOISTS
SPIT	TETHERED	FREE SPACE	RACUOUS	COAXED
RESTIVE	MAGNANIMOUSLY	PENCE	SCORN	BRIDLE
SAGEBRUSH	DEFIANT	IMPERIOUSLY	TRANSFUSION	MULISH

Indian In The Cupboard Vocab

UNWARILY	FOREBODING	SAGEBRUSH	RAPTURE	COHERENT
MAGNANIMOUSLY	SCALPS	RANSACKED	DEFIANT	GALVANIZED
OBLIGED	PETRIFIED	FREE SPACE	DISMAY	DESPAIR
MYRIAD	APPALLED	PENCE	FIENDISH	SEPTIC
APPREHENSION	HECTORING	OMNIVOROUS	TACTICS	JOISTS

Indian In The Cupboard Vocab

MINUTE	INCREDULOUS	BEMUSED	INFURIATED	TOURNIQUET
TRUCE	BAFFLEMENT	PEEVISHLY	RELAPSE	BRIDLE
SNIDE	TRANSFUSION	FREE SPACE	RACUOUS	TETHERED
BANDOLIER	VULNERABLE	COAXED	SCORN	LITHELY
PERILS	RELUCTANT	MAIZE	SPIT	AGHAST

Indian In The Cupboard Vocab

HECTORING	FOREBODING	RAPTURE	IMPERIOUSLY	DEFIANT
TOURNIQUET	OBLIGED	AGHAST	SCORN	BRIDLE
MAGNANIMOUSLY	MYRIAD	FREE SPACE	TETHERED	LONGHOUSE
INTRICATE	APPREHENSION	COHERENT	DISMAY	FIENDISH
OMNIVOROUS	SCALPS	PENCE	SEPTIC	RESTIVE

Indian In The Cupboard Vocab

BANDOLIER	SNIDE	MINUTE	BAFFLEMENT	LITHELY
INCREDULOUS	TRUCE	COAXED	SAGEBRUSH	TACTICS
RELAPSE	TRANSFIXED	FREE SPACE	RANSACKED	JOISTS
RACUOUS	RAVENOUSLY	PEEVISHLY	APPALLED	GAPED
PETRIFIED	RETORTED	PERILS	PERSECUTOR	GALVANIZED

Indian In The Cupboard Vocab

DEFIANT	SCORN	SCALPS	DESPAIR	HECTORING
GALVANIZED	UNWARILY	RELAPSE	TRANSFIXED	VULNERABLE
PENCE	RETORTED	FREE SPACE	INFURIATED	PEEVISHLY
TACTICS	GAPED	SNIDE	RESTIVE	MULISH
REGRETFULLY	MINUTE	RACUOUS	SAGEBRUSH	SEPTIC

Indian In The Cupboard Vocab

TOURNIQUET	RANSACKED	JOISTS	MYRIAD	COAXED
TRANSFUSION	PETRIFIED	MAGNANIMOUSLY	INTRICATE	RAVENOUSLY
SPIT	LITHELY	FREE SPACE	TRUCE	MAIZE
APPREHENSION	OMNIVOROUS	RAPTURE	PERILS	INCREDULOUS
COHERENT	BAFFLEMENT	BRIDLE	FIENDISH	AGHAST

Indian In The Cupboard Vocab

RELUCTANT	TETHERED	FOREBODING	GALVANIZED	INFURIATED
DISMAY	TOURNIQUET	MULISH	LITHELY	RELAPSE
TACTICS	FLUMMOXED	FREE SPACE	SAGEBRUSH	SPIT
OBLIGED	DESPAIR	TRANSFIXED	PERSECUTOR	IMPERIOUSLY
RAVENOUSLY	INTRICATE	MAGNANIMOUSLY	UNWARILY	RACUOUS

Indian In The Cupboard Vocab

APPALLED	BRIDLE	HECTORING	LONGHOUSE	BEMUSED
GAPED	MYRIAD	RETORTED	BANDOLIER	INCREDULOUS
REGRETFULLY	PENCE	FREE SPACE	COAXED	JOISTS
FIENDISH	PETRIFIED	RAPTURE	SCORN	BAFFLEMENT
TRUCE	DEFIANT	MINUTE	MAIZE	SNIDE